The Silk Road A Journey Through History

Rajesh Gupta

Copyright © [2023]

Author: The Silk Road A Journey Through History
Title: Rajesh Gupta

All rights reserved. No part of this book may be reproduced or transmitted in any form or by any means, electronic or mechanical, including photocopying, recording, or by any information storage and retrieval system, without permission in writing from the author.

This book is a product of

ISBN:

Table of content

Chapter Name   **Page No**

1. An Outline of the Silk Road — 1
2. Routes of Ancient Commerce — 14
3. Silk Road's Infancy — 25
4. Silk and spices: Silk Road wares — 35
5. Cultural and Religious Globalisation — 43
6. The Mighty Empires of the Silk Road — 51
7. The heyday of the Silk Road — 59
8. Problems and Difficulties — 68
9. Fall and History — 78
10. Revival and rediscovery — 88
11. Conclusion — 98
12. Extra Materials — 106

Chapter 1.
An Outline of the Silk Road

1.1- Brief overview of the Silk Road's significance

The Silk Road: A Legendary Route for the Exchange of Goods, Ideas, and Cultures

There will always be a place in history for the Silk Road, the historic network of interconnecting trade routes that stretched over Asia, Europe, and Africa. Over the course of more than two millennia, this extensive network of roads was used by merchants, adventurers, and intellectuals to facilitate a spectacular exchange of products, ideas, and civilizations. The Silk Road, which began in Han Dynasty China and ended in the Roman Empire, was more than just a commercial highway; it was a link between cultures that ushered in societal change and ultimately helped create the modern world.

We will embark on a multifaceted investigation of the Silk Road's historical significance, learning about its economic, cultural, and intellectual effects. This story intends to provide readers a thorough grasp of how the Silk Road influenced the development of human civilisation from its inception to the present day.

The First Steps on the Silk Road

During the Western Han Dynasty (206 BCE - 220 CE) in China, Emperor Wu Di sent an emissary by the name of Zhang Qian to the western provinces, marking the beginning of the Silk Road. Zhang Qian was sent to make connections with faraway people and learn more about the world outside China's borders. Zhang Qian found a wealth of treasures and learned about many cultures that the Chinese had never heard of during his travels.

Silk, a magnificent cloth, was one of the most sought-after items Zhang Qian came across in the West. The Chinese had kept their silk production method a closely guarded secret for generations. It wasn't until Zhang Qian's journeys that silk began its famed westward voyage.

The Commercial Routes of the Silk Road:

The Silk Road was not just one route, but rather a web of several routes connecting different countries. Some of the most important sections of the Silk Road were:

1. The Northern Way This path left from China, traversed Central Asia, and ended up in the Black Sea and the Mediterranean by way of the Ferghana Valley and the towns of Samarkand and Bukhara.

Second, the Southern Way : If you wished to bypass Central Asia's rough terrain, this was an option. It originated in India and continued across modern-day Iran and the Arabian Peninsula to the western edge of the Roman Empire.

Third, the Maritime Route: The Maritime Silk Road was a network of sea lanes that extended from China to Southeast Asia, India, and beyond. It aided in the transport of valuables including spices, gems, and textiles.

The Eastern Way (4) Cultural exchange between East Asian countries was encouraged by this fork in the Silk Road that linked China to Korea and Japan.

Weather, political stability, and market demand all had a role in how these routes were used by merchants. Therefore, the Silk Road was a developing network that connected many different cultures.

Items sold along the Silk Road:

The Silk Road was used to interchange a wide variety of items, the most well-known of which was probably silk. What was traded along the Silk Road?

1. Silk: Silk was so highly regarded in the West that it inspired the Silk Road. The fabric was coveted for its luxurious feel, luxurious gloss, and rarity.

Spices, secondly: Spices like cinnamon, pepper, and cloves were brought to the West by way of the Silk Road, which had a profound impact on Western cooking.

Precious Metals and Gemstones, No. 3: Along these channels circulated precious metals and stones used as cash and as status symbols, including gold, silver, and jewels like turquoise, lapis lazuli, and jade.

[4] [T]extiles: Silk was just one of several textiles that were traded frequently.

5. Tea: After being exported from China, tea quickly became a staple in countries across Central Asia and beyond.

6. Paper: The discovery of paper in China greatly aided the spread of knowledge and information, as it allowed for the convenient transfer of written materials such as manuscripts and texts.

The delicate beauty and long-lasting quality of fine Chinese porcelain made it a highly sought-after commodity in the West.

Objects of exotic value (ivory, incense, and animals): Due to their uniqueness and exoticism, these goods were in high demand.

Religious Icons and Symbolism 9 Religious art and iconography from Buddhism, Islam, and Christianity made their way over the Silk Road.

Medicinal plants and information, number 10. As a result of these interactions, diverse regions were able to benefit from the interchange of traditional medicine and knowledge systems.

The exchange of these items benefited not only the merchants themselves, but also the societies and cultures they went through.

Cultural blending and mutual influence:

The Silk Road was notable for the amount of cultural interaction that took place along its paths. Along with their wares, merchants, pilgrims, and students brought with them new ideas, religious practises, and aesthetic canons.

Religion first: The dissemination of religion was greatly aided by the Silk Road. Along these trade routes, the Indian religion of Buddhism spread to the lands of Central Asia and East Asia. Similar to the spread of Buddhism throughout China and the rest of Asia, the spread of Zoroastrianism, Nestorian Christianity, and Islam also occurred.

Second, The Arts: The evolution of unique regional art forms was facilitated by the sharing of styles and methods amongst artists. Central Asian art and architecture, for instance, is distinguished by a synthesis of Persian and Chinese styles.

Thirdly, Writing Systems and Languages: Along the Silk Road, people were forced to learn and use new languages and writing systems as a means of communication and documentation. For example, the Uighur script, which is widely used in Central Asia, evolved from the Sogdian script.

4. Cuisine: Fusion cuisines emerged as spices, cooking methods, and ingredients from various cultures mingled.

5. Science and Medicine: As a result of the free exchange of ideas between civilizations, scientific and medical developments were made in astronomy, mathematics, and medicine.

Hybrid cultures emerged in many parts of the world as a result of the mixing and matching of ideas and practises from different parts of the world, creating a rich tapestry of human civilisation.

Effects on Superpowers and Nation-States

The Silk Road had far-reaching consequences for the states and empires along its route. It was crucial in the formation of major trading hubs, the growth of empires, and the spread of political systems.

Han Dynasty, No. 1: Since it was during the Han Dynasty that China first made contact with Central Asia and the West, this period is often considered to be synonymous with the birth of the Silk Road. The Han Dynasty grew powerful and influential thanks to the Silk Road's economic benefits.

Silk and other luxury products were in high demand in Roman society, and this contributed greatly to the growth of the Silk Road. As a result, the Romans were exposed to new ideas and aesthetics from the Far East.

The Byzantine Empire, Number Three: After the fall of the Roman Empire, the Byzantines continued the Silk Road's extensive trade with the Far East. It facilitated the flow of information and trade between the East and the West.

The Mongol Empire was a massive empire that existed during the

Safe passage for traders along the Silk Road was ensured by powerful leaders like Genghis Khan and Kublai Khan. The result was the Pax Mongolica, a period of extraordinary commercial and cultural interaction between the two regions.

5. The Caliphate States of Islam: The Islamic world, especially during the Abbasid Caliphate, was instrumental in the success of Silk Road commerce. Knowledge from Greek, Persian, and Indian sources was transmitted to the West thanks to the translation activity in Baghdad.

Central Asian empires such as the Kushan Empire, the Sogdian city-states, and the Timurid Empire flourished along the Silk Road because of their central location.

The Silk Road's existence often played a key part in moulding the destinies of empires, and its rise and fall were intertwined with its fortunes.

What Caused the Silk Road to Fade?

There were hiccups along the Silk Road. Over the centuries, it declined due to a number of factors:

1. The Fall of the Mongols: As the Mongol Empire fell apart, the peace and safety it had brought to the Silk Road began to deteriorate.

2. Change in Commercial Paths During the 15th century, when the Age of Exploration began and sea channels were opened, maritime trade grew in importance, taking business away from the land-based Silk Road.

Political Unrest: Political unpredictability, such as invasions, battles, and the growth of isolationist attitudes in some regions, frequently disrupted Silk Road trade.

More efficient and modern modes of transportation, such as ocean-going ships and railroads, reduced the appeal of trading across land.

Despite all of these obstacles, the Silk Road survived. It morphed and altered, so that some parts of the route are still in use today to carry goods and people from one place to another.

The Lasting Impact of the Silk Road:

Although the historic Silk Road trade routes are no longer the major means of transporting goods throughout the world, their influence is nevertheless seen in many ways today.

First, Cultural Interaction: The Silk Road left a mark in the form of cultural diversity as a result of centuries of trade and exchange.

2. Economic Integration: The idea of linking geographically disparate regions through commercial exchange continues to be a primary force in promoting worldwide economic integration.

Thirdly, "Technology Transfer" Along the Silk Road, people were able to share their knowledge and ideas, paving the way for future scientific advancements.

Diplomacy and Global Politics, Number Four Corridors once traversed by the Silk Road remain significant in modern geopolitics due to their historical role in fostering diplomatic ties between governments and influencing geopolitical strategy.

5. Education and Tourism Today, visitors and academics alike go to the districts along the ancient Silk Road pathways to learn more about the region's fascinating past and fascinating culture.

By enhancing communication and commerce between Asia, Europe, and Africa, modern infrastructure projects like China's Belt and Road Initiative (BRI) want to reawaken interest in the ancient Silk Road.

Artefacts from the Silk Road are important, but the intangible cultural, intellectual, and cooperative ties that were established along the route are what will ultimately ensure the road's lasting legacy.

Conclusion:

The Silk Road is evidence of humanity's incredible ability to bridge disparate cultures and regions. Over the course of more than two thousand years, it facilitated the movement of goods, ideas, and cultures between different parts of the world, ultimately changing the trajectory of human history. The Silk Road served as a conduit for the exchange of everything from fine Chinese silk to fragrant Indian spices, from the teachings of ancient philosophers to the tenets of emerging religions.Looking back, we can see that the Silk Road's legacy is still there in today's interconnected globe. It serves as a timely reminder that the ties of commerce, culture, and mutual understanding may break down artificial barriers to create a more interdependent and peaceful global community.

In this epic trip through the Silk Road's significance, we have traced its origins, investigated its various trade routes, dove deeply into the cultural interchange it facilitated, examined the impact it had on empires, and seen how it has changed and what legacy it has left behind. Stories of the Silk Road's exploration, connection, and building of bridges across our own modern issues and divisions continue to inspire us because of this.

1.2- Geographical layout of the Silk Road

The Silk Road's Detailed Map: A Woven Network of Connections

The legendary Silk Road, which linked Asia and Europe in antiquity, was not a straight line but rather a dynamic network of passageways. Because of the wide variety of terrains and ecosystems it passed through, the region's geography was like a tapestry, providing a colourful and exciting experience for businesspeople, explorers, and vacationers alike. This paper will examine the Silk Road's geographical layout, touching on the areas it traversed and the opportunities and perils encountered by its travellers.

The Orient: Ancient China

China, the original starting point of the Silk Road, was the farthest point east. The "Silk Route," as the Chinese leg of the Silk Road was known, began in Chang'an (present-day Xi'an). It then spread out in several different directions.

The Northerly Way There was a fork on the Silk Road that went north of the Taklamakan Desert and into the fruitful Hexi Corridor. The Gobi Desert to the north and the Tibetan Plateau to the south created a narrow passageway that was generally safe for travellers.

The Southern Way An alternate southern fork avoided the severe deserts by passing via the Tarim Basin's oasis and then followed the foothills of the Himalayas to Central Asia, where it connected with the northern route. This path south provided welcome relief from the harsh desert climate.

Central Asia is a strategic hub.

Trade and cultural interaction flourished along the Silk Road, which had its epicentre in Central Asia. The large area that is now the countries of Kazakhstan, Uzbekistan, Turkmenistan, Tajikistan, and Kyrgyzstan was home to a wide range of landscapes, including but not limited to the following.

Deserts: Both the Kyzylkum and Karakum deserts presented significant challenges to traders. Merv, a historic city on the edge of the Karakum Desert, served as a major transportation and commercial centre.

Oases: Samarkand, Bukhara, and Khiva served as oasis cities along the Silk Road, where weary travellers and merchants could stop and replenish their supplies.

Mountainous Landscape: The Tien Shan and Pamir Mountains presented difficulties but also provided rare metals and jewels.

Western Asia is the "Door to Europe."

Moving further west, the Silk Road eventually reached modern-day Iran, Iraq, and the Middle East. The cities and cultural history along this stretch of the Silk Road were legendary.

Iran: The ancient Persian Empire, centred on the city of Persepolis, was an important stop along the Silk Road. The Silk Road was modelled by a previous trading route, the Persian Royal Road.

Mesopotamia: Mesopotamian cities like Babylon and Ur had a long history of serving as crossroads for traders from the East and West.

Turkey and Syria: Damascus and Antioch, both important stops along the Silk Road, were located in this region. This point is important since it is where the Silk Road's westernmost branch meets the Mediterranean.

The Mediterranean Sea, the Westernmost Point on Earth

The Mediterranean Sea was the endpoint of the Silk Road in the west and a major entry point to Europe. Many of the Silk Road's most prized items were destined for the Mediterranean region, which included ancient Rome, Greece, and Byzantium (modern-day Istanbul):

The Empire of Rome: Silk, spices, and other luxury goods were in high demand in Rome, which contributed to the growth of the Silk Road trade route. Rome itself was an important stop along the Silk Road, where exotic goods from the East were welcomed.

Sea of the Red: Goods could be delivered from the East to the Mediterranean via safer sea routes via ports like Alexandria and Myos Hormos on the Red Sea.

The Southern Link to Africa

Although most travel along the Silk Road took place on land, there were also sea routes that linked Asia and Africa. Trade between Africa and the Silk Road was facilitated in part by ancient ports along the Red Sea and Indian Ocean coasts, such as Aden and Zanzibar.

Subcontinent of India: A Branch of the Silk Road

The modern-day countries of India, Pakistan, and Bangladesh were part of an independent network of trade routes that linked to the Silk Road. Goods like as textiles, spices, and jewels were traded between South Asia and the remainder of the Silk Road along these pathways.

Opportunities and Threats on the Silk Road

The Silk Road's route network presented its travellers with a unique set of obstacles and opportunities:

Extremely Dry Regions: Central Asia's deserts posed significant challenges, especially the Taklamakan and Gobi regions. Extreme heat, shifting sands, and a shortage of water and shelter were just some of the challenges that travellers faced.

Seasonal Mountain Permits: Dangerous terrain and shifting weather patterns were features unique to the mountainous regions of the Tien Shan and Pamir Mountains. On the other hand, these regions had an abundance of resources.

Oases: The oasis towns along the Silk Road were vital stops for tired caravans, offering shelter, water, and supplies. Oases like these quickly developed as commercial and cultural hubs.

Culture to Culture Contact: Cultural interchange occurred along the Silk Road because of the variety of landscapes and locations. Those who traded and travelled between regions were exposed to new cultures, religions, and languages. This free flow of information and ideas was a defining feature of the Silk Road.

Commercial Activity: The Silk Road's strategic placement resulted in a massive trading hub where Eastern and Western products met. The exchange of goods and services boosted economies all around the world.

Transferring Technology: Innovating was another response to the difficulties of the Silk Road. Long-distance desert travel, for instance, relied on the development of the camel saddle, which in turn relied on reliable desert navigation.

Geography's Silk Road Heritage

The Silk Road's geographic pattern permanently altered the places it passed through:

Cultural Differences: The Silk Road's varied landscapes helped foster the complex mosaic of civilizations that developed along its paths. It encouraged the communication of ideas and the dissemination of cultural practises.

Construction in Urban Areas: As a result of their strategic location along the Silk Road, the cities and oasis towns there prospered. The Silk Road's influence is still felt today in cities like Samarkand, Bukhara, Xi'an, and many others.

Technological and Scientific Progress: The obstacles presented by the Silk Road's terrain prompted new approaches to travel, navigation, and building.

Important Historical Sites: The Silk Road left an indelible effect on history, as seen by numerous relics from China's Great Wall to Jordan's ancient city of Petra.

Contemporary Linking The spirit of the Silk Road lives on in modern initiatives like China's Belt and Road Initiative, which aim to improve communication and commerce along ancient trading routes.

To sum up, the Silk Road's physical layout was a complex and complicated web that allowed for the free flow of goods, ideas, and cultures between the East and the West. It was a trip through a wide variety of scenery, from the mountains of Central Asia to the thriving metropolises of the Mediterranean. The enduring significance of the Silk Road attests to the

human curiosity, commerce, and cultural exchange has inspired people for millennia, and it continues to fuel our efforts to break down barriers in today's globe.

Chapter 2.
Routes of Ancient Commerce

2.1- Exploration of early trade routes that predated the Silk Road

Investigation of Pre-Silk Road Trade Routes

Even before the Silk Road became the most famous network of trade routes in history, people all over the world were actively trading with one another and exchanging ideas and cultural practises. These pre-Silk Road trade routes helped pave the way for the later network and had a significant impact on the development of human society. Discover the significance and global influence of these historic trade routes as you embark on this journey of discovery.

Connecting the North through the Amber Road.

The Amber Road was among the oldest and best-known of Europe's ancient trading routes. This path, which preceded the Silk Road by several centuries, linked the northern Baltic Sea with the southern Mediterranean Sea. Amber, the region's most valuable export, inspired the city's name.

Overview of the Route: Through modern-day Poland, Germany, Austria, and Italy, the Amber Road covered a great deal of ground. Amber was mostly mined along the Baltic Sea shore, specifically in what is today's Lithuania.

Primary Materials While amber was the route's most valuable product, furs, lumber, and metallurgy were also exchanged. Amber was valued for more than just its aesthetic value in the marketplace; it was also used as an amulet and in jewellery.

Culture to Culture Contact: The Amber Road connected northern and southern Europe culturally. Along with their wares, traders and travellers brought new ideas and customs to the table.

Impact: Cities along the Amber Road benefited from its growth, and the culture of the regions it linked was influenced by it. Like the Silk Road in Asia, it allowed for the free exchange of goods and information.

The Incense Trade: Bringing Ancient Scents to the Modern World.

The Incense Route was a series of commercial routes that spanned from modern-day Yemen in southern Arabia to the Mediterranean Sea. Its most famous export, incense, inspired the name of the city.

Overview of the Route: The ancient cities of Shabwah, Marib, and Sanaa were all on the Incense Route's path across the Arabian Peninsula. Going north through the desert, it eventually reached Petra in Jordan and Gaza in Palestine. Egypt and other Mediterranean countries were also accessible by sea routes.

Primary Materials Incense, such as frankincense and myrrh, was the main product exchanged along the Incense Route. Fragrances like these were greatly sought after for their usage in perfumes, incense, and even medicinal preparations.

Culture to Culture Contact: Not only were items traded along the Incense Route, but so were ideas about religion and culture. Whether it was the worship of Arabian deities or the doctrines of early Christianity, it was crucial in the dissemination of Arabian culture and religions.

Impact: The Arabian Peninsula grew rich thanks to incense trading along the Incense Route. Important ancient civilizations like the

Sabaeans and the Nabateans rose to prominence as a result of their control of strategic points along the route.

Crossing the African Desert on the Trans-Saharan Trade Routes

The Trans-Saharan trade routes played a crucial role in linking North Africa with sub-Saharan Africa in the African interior. Gold, salt, and other precious metals, as well as exotic products, were traded along these routes.

Overview of the Route: Large swaths of the Sahara Desert were traversed by the Trans-Saharan trade routes that linked countries as diverse as Morocco, Tunisia, and Egypt with Mali, Ghana, and Nigeria. The desert was crisscrossed by caravan routes that connected various markets and oasis towns.

Primary Materials Two primary goods, gold from sub-Saharan Africa and salt from the Sahara, dominated the trading routes. These were extremely important commodities, and the commerce in them propelled the economies of the regions along the routes.

Culture to Culture Contact: As well as products, culture, language, and religion were all freely traded over the Trans-Saharan routes. For instance, Islam moved southward via these corridors.

Impact: The establishment of mighty West African dynasties like Ghana, Mali, and Songhai, who dominated significant parts of the commerce, was made possible by these routes. This commerce brought in a lot of money, which was used to build some really fantastic stuff like cities and monuments.

Ancient Flavours from Around the World

The Silk Road was developed centuries after the Spice Route and Spice Trade, although both served to facilitate commerce between

East and West. It got its name because exotic spices were big business there.

Overview of the Route: India, Southeast Asia, Arabia, and the Mediterranean were all linked via the Spice Route, which included both sea and land routes. Calicut (in India), Malacca (in Malaysia), and Alexandria (in Egypt) were all significant stops along the sea routes.

Primary Materials The principal goods trafficked along the Spice Route were spices including pepper, cinnamon, cloves, and nutmeg. In addition to their culinary value, these spices have medical, religious, and preservation applications.

Culture to Culture Contact: Cultures and ideas met and mingled along the Spice Route. Not just spices, but also cloth, pottery, ideas, and art were traded thanks to this route.

Impact: The rise of several empires, including the Roman and Byzantine ones, can be traced back to the Spice Route. The increasing demand for spices in the 15th century encouraged European powers to seek for new ways to the Spice Islands, kicking off the Age of Exploration.

Exchange Networks Before the Silk Road

While the Silk Road is certainly worthy of praise, it is important not to gloss over the extensive and varied history of commerce that came before it. The modern global economy can be traced back to ancient trade routes such as the Amber Road, the Incense Route, the Trans-Saharan trade routes, and the Spice Route.

Culture to Culture Contact: These pathways for commerce served as thoroughfares for the dissemination of ideas as well. They connected people from different cultures, resulting in a mingling of languages, beliefs, and customs.

Expansion of the Economy: Trade along these routes fueled the growth of thriving communities and expansive empires. Cities expanded, infrastructure was built, and money was amassed thanks to it.

Science and Technology Cooperation: Cultures exchanged not only things but also information when they came into contact with one another. Ideas were shared in areas as diverse as medicine, astronomy, and mathematics.

Spiritual and Religious Communication: Along these pathways, people also spread their religious ideas and rituals. Religions like Buddhism, Christianity, and Islam were able to expand around the world because of the free flow of people and ideas.

An Exploration Legacy These early commercial channels were crucial in defining the course of exploration. Explorers were motivated to discover new places and things by their desire to acquire riches, such as spices and precious metals.

Finally, the Silk Road's predecessors have been discovered to indicate a complex web of human contact, exchange, and invention. These pathways, which spanned continents and centuries, brought together previously isolated communities and enriched them culturally, economically, and intellectually. The Silk Road is the most well-known of these historic trade routes, yet it is only one chapter in a much larger story of global interchange that has had a significant impact on our modern world.

2.2- How silk and other goods influenced ancient

The Role of Silk and Other Products in the Development of Early Economies

Silk and other exotic items have been among the most influential and desirable goods in economic history. Silk's luxurious shine and smooth feel made it more than just a fabric—it was a status symbol. Silk wasn't the only commodity that was crucial to the development of ancient economies; spices, precious metals, jewels, and textiles also played important roles. In this investigation, we look at how silk and various other goods altered ancient economies.

Silk: It's Fit for a King's Cloak

The history of silk, which comes from the cocoon of the silkworm, dates back more than 5,000 years to ancient China. Silk was one of the most prized commodities for millennia, and the Chinese jealously guarded their production techniques.

Manufacturing and Commerce: This rich fabric was tightly controlled by ancient China due to its production monopoly. The manufacturing of silk was a governmental secret that carried the death penalty if revealed. As a result, China maintained a de facto monopoly on silk production for hundreds of years, keeping the fabric's value and demand high.

Economic Consequences In ancient China, silk manufacture was a major source of income. Many people were put to work in the silk business, from farmers of silkworms to weavers, dyers, and merchants. The increasing need for silk not only boosted the economy, but also helped pave the way for better transportation and communication systems.

Diplomacy and Silk: The ancient Chinese government's diplomatic efforts included the symbolic exchange of silk as a gesture of goodwill, known as "silk diplomacy." Diplomatic ties were strengthened and commerce deals were made through the exchange of silken gifts.

Commercial Routes: China's silk commerce spanned continents. Silk and other items were traded between the East and the West thanks to the Silk Road, a network of interconnected trade routes. Along these corridors, silk was shipped as far as the Roman Empire.

Repercussions on Western Economies The economic impact of silk's introduction to the West was substantial. Importing silk from China resulted in large sums of Roman cash leaving the country. In an effort to slow these outflows, Roman senators proposed a law restricting the use of silk.

The Spices of International Business

In ancient times, spices like pepper, cinnamon, cloves, and nutmeg were highly prized possessions. They were used for seasoning, preserving meat, healing, and rituals.

Sources: India, Sri Lanka, the Spice Islands (present-day Indonesia), and the Malabar Coast were among the most important spice-producing locales. These areas soon became important centres for the production and distribution of spices.

Commercial Routes: The spice trade involved multiple pathways, both land and sea. From Asia to the Mediterranean, spices were transported over land routes such as the Incense Route and the Silk Road. Spices might be shipped via the water because of maritime routes like the Spice Route.

Profitability under Monopoly: Spice monopolies and huge profits were common results of this control. There was a lot of rivalry in the ancient spice trade since so many different emperors and merchant organisations wanted to dominate the spice-growing regions.

Consequences for Ancient Economies: Spices were highly prized for their medicinal and preservational benefits in addition to their culinary purposes. Spice consumption fueled expansion, facilitated commerce, and encouraged discovery.

Gold, silver, and gems all serve as status symbols

Gold, silver, turquoise, lapis lazuli, and jade are just a few examples of the precious metals and gemstones that have been prized by humans since prehistoric times. The wealth, power, and reputation they represented were reflected in the value of these commodities.

Mining and Commerce: The gold mines of Nubia and the silver mines of Laurion in ancient Greece are only two examples of specialised mining regions for these precious metals. However, gemstones came from all over the world, including Afghanistan and India.

Financial Structures Many early forms of currency were based on precious metals. Metal coins like gold and silver dollars made it easier to do business. These coins' purity and weight were crucial for building confidence in commerce.

Consequences for Ancient Economies: Ancient civilizations' ability to accumulate precious metals and gemstones, and hence mint coins, contributed to their overall economic might. These coins, displaying the images of kings and gods, were vital to commerce.

From Cotton to Linen and Beyond

Many ancient societies' economics relied heavily on textile production, which included cotton, wool, linen, and other fibres. Agriculture, animal husbandry, spinning, weaving, and dying were all necessary steps in the textile production process.

Sources: Where textiles came from changed from region to region. The Indian subcontinent and the Middle East were major producers of cotton, while sheep were the primary source of wool. Ancient Egyptians made extensive use of linen, a fabric manufactured from flax.

Commercial Activity: Fabrics served several roles outside clothing, including sails, tents, and awnings. There was a flourishing economy because of the textile industry, which included artisans, weavers, and traders.

Evolutions in Technology: Looms, spinning wheels, and new dyeing processes were all inventions made possible by the textile industry. The productivity and quality of textile manufacturing were both raised by these developments.

Consequences for Ancient Economies: There were many people who were able to support themselves and their families because of the textile industry. Growth, commerce, and the establishment of major trading hubs were all spurred on by the textile industry.

Culture and Society as Affected by Rare Items

Silk, spices, precious metals, and textiles were not only important economically, but also culturally and socially in ancient communities.

Luxury and social standing: Possession of these unusual items was a mark of affluence and sophistication. Silk, spices, and expensive textiles were signs of wealth and social status, therefore its owners were typically looked up to.

Culture to Culture Contact: Cultural interaction was promoted by the exchange of these products. Cultural exchange and mutual enrichment were fostered through the introduction of novel foods, building materials, and forms of expression.

Ceremonial and Religious Significance: Many unusual items, such spices and valuable metals, were used in rituals and ceremonies. They were presented as gifts and depicted in religious artefacts and rites.

Craftsmanship and the Fine Arts: Traditions of art and craftsmanship flourished in response to the need for unusual commodities. Craftsmen and jewellers used these components in elaborate patterns and motifs.

Research and Development: The need to find new and different things fueled exploration and new discoveries. Risky expeditions were undertaken by explorers and merchants in pursuit of these goods.

Heritage in the Contemporary World

Silk and other exotic items left an indelible mark on ancient civilizations, one that is still felt today.

Importance in Cultural Terms: The cultural significance of silk, spices, precious metals, and textiles has persisted in many countries. They have deep roots in customs and ceremonies that mark special occasions.

International Business: The early development of global commerce networks was propelled by the need for these products. Commodity exchanges, such those for textiles and spices, are still vital to the modern economy.

Influence in the Market One of the most important factors in the rise and fall of ancient empires was the acquisition of wealth through the exchange of exotic items. One of the most important factors in contemporary geopolitics is economic might.

Aesthetics and Dress: The artistic and artisanal practises that developed in response to these products live on today.

to have an impact on modern aesthetics and production.

In conclusion, ancient economies relied heavily on the production, trade, and consumption of luxury goods including silk, spices, precious metals, jewels, and textiles. These rare items impacted global communication, economic systems, and the rise of entire cultures. Their influence can still be felt today in the forms taken by cultural norms, international commerce, and national economies.

Chapter 3.
Silk Road's Infancy

3.1- Historical context and the Silk Road's origins

Origins of the Silk Road and Its Role in History

The Silk Road did not develop in a vacuum; it was part of a larger system of ancient trade routes that linked East and West. It resulted from the interplay of several factors in its time and place, including politics, culture, technology, and geography. Explore the historical context that laid the groundwork for the Silk Road's colossal trade of products, ideas, and cultures.

The Beginnings: Trade Before the Silk Road

The early attempts at commercial trade laid the groundwork for what would become the Silk Road. Many distinct routes and roads were already in use for commerce between various regions and civilizations before the Silk Road was formally established. The more organised and extensive Silk Road that eventually emerged had its origins in these early trading routes.

First, The Incense Trail: Trading fragrant resins and spices began along the Incense Route between southern Arabia and the Mediterranean as early as 2000 BCE. This path established a standard for long-distance trade and inspired the eventual construction of the Silk Road.

The Royal Route 2. The Royal Road was built by Darius the Great during the fifth century BCE and connected the cities of Susa and Sardis in the Persian Empire. It was a system of well-kept highways and communication hubs where goods and information could be exchanged.

Third, "Trade in the Indian Ocean" Seaborne routes linked the Indian subcontinent to neighbouring regions in East Africa and Southeast Asia. Merchandise, ideas, and even faiths were all able to be freely traded thanks to these pathways.

Empires rose to power and paved the way for commerce.

The emergence and growth of empires were crucial in laying the groundwork for the Silk Road. Trade was facilitated under imperial rule because of the political stability it offered. There were three major empires that played significant roles in the development of the Silk Road:

The Persian Empire, No. The Achaemenid dynasty built a massive and interconnected network of roadways throughout the Persian Empire, one of which was the Royal Road. The infrastructure was a huge help in facilitating trade and communication throughout the empire.

2. The Empire of the Mauryas The Maurya Empire (4th-2nd century BCE) consolidated power in ancient India and encouraged commercial and industrial development. Pataliputra, the empire's capital, flourished as a commercial and diplomatic centre.

Third, during the Han Dynasty: Trade along the Silk Road was made possible during the Han Dynasty (206 BCE – 220 CE) in China. The Chinese government encouraged commerce, regulated its currency, and protected traders along its trade routes.

The Developments in Technology Have Made Long-Distance Commerce Possible.

A significant factor in the formation of the Silk Road was the advancement of technology and innovations. Several significant technological developments facilitated long-distance trade:

First, the Camel Saddle: Desert travel was greatly aided by the taming of camels and the development of the camel saddle. The deserts of the Silk Road were ideal for camel travel because of their great distances and ability to carry huge goods.

2. Paper: During the Han Dynasty in China, paper was invented, and it immediately changed the way messages were sent and kept. Keeping records of business dealings and communicating with government officials was simplified.

Thirdly, the Compass and the Astrolabe facilitated advancements in maritime navigation. These tools improved navigational accuracy for mariners, which boosted commerce along sea routes.

Cultural Interaction as a Driving Force on the Silk Road.

While things were traded, ideas, culture, and religion also flowed freely over the Silk Road. The historical setting of the Silk Road facilitated cultural interaction:

First, the Spread of Religions Buddhism, Islam, Christianity, Zoroastrianism, and other religions were all disseminated with the help of the Silk Road. Along these paths, religious leaders, monks, and academics spread their beliefs and knowledge to new areas.

Writing and Language 2. Language and writing systems sprang out along the Silk Road because of the demand for communication. Examples of this linguistic interaction include the development of the Chinese writing system throughout East Asia and the introduction of Indian scripts to Southeast Asia.

Cultural Exchange in the Arts (3): Craftsmen and builders who plied their trade along the Silk Road were influenced by a wide range of cultural traditions. As a result of these interactions, new aesthetic trends, architectural plans, and complex works of art emerged.

The Development of the Silk Road: An Interconnected Chain

The development of the Silk Road was not a sudden occurrence but rather a gradual, multi-stage process that unfolded over the course of centuries. It was shaped by a number of influences working together:

First, Geographical Considerations: The Silk Road's routes and destinations were impacted by the landscapes through which it passed, from the harsh deserts of Central Asia to the rich oases and mountain passes.

Economic Requirements Merchants and traders were motivated to seek out and build new routes by the high demand for luxury commodities like silk and spices, as well as the opportunity for financial gain.

Political Stability (3): The presence of empires and states that provided security and infrastructure along trade routes facilitated economic development.

Long-distance commerce became more practical and lucrative as a result of technological advancements in transportation, navigation, and communication.

Five, Cultural Interactions: Cultures all along the Silk Road's path were enriched by the free flow of ideas, beliefs, and artistic expressions.

The Historical Roots of the Silk Road's Establishment

Historical factors such as established trade routes, the security afforded by empires, technological advancements, and the desire for cultural and commercial exchange all contributed to the development of the Silk Road. It was a symbol of human inventiveness, ambition, and the desire to make contact with people and places far away from where they lived.

As it grew and changed, the Silk Road became a symbol of global connectivity, bridging Asia, the Middle East, and beyond through commerce, diplomacy, cultural diffusion, and the sharing of information. It left an indelible impression on global history and is a tribute to the perseverance of the human spirit of exploration, cooperation, and cultural exchange.

3.2- Key figures and civilizations involved in its creation

Culture, invention, and cooperation have all contributed to the tapestry that is human history. As we explore our common history, we find that many different cultures and individuals had significant impacts on the modern world. These influential people and societies have left their impact on the course of human history from the earliest known civilizations in Mesopotamia and Egypt to the Renaissance in Europe and the current globalised globe.

Cradle of Civilization refers to Mesopotamia.

Many consider Mesopotamia, a region commonly called the "Cradle of Civilization," to be one of the most significant places in human history. Some of the earliest known civilizations emerged in the lush crescent between the Tigris and Euphrates rivers. It was at this time that Hammurabi, the sixth monarch of the First Babylonian Dynasty, made his mark. The Code of Hammurabi, which he authored, is one of the earliest legal laws in human history and will be remembered for this reason. Inscribed on a stone tablet, this code provided a foundation for law and justice, centering on maxims like "an eye for an eye."

Even before Hammurabi's Babylonians, the ancient Sumerians had made great strides in human progress. They are recognised as the creators of cuneiform, one of the oldest writing systems. This development was a watershed moment in human intellectual progress since it made possible the recording of sacred materials such as laws and religious writings as well as historical narratives.

The Pharaonic Empire of Ancient Egypt

Ancient Egypt was a lynchpin of early culture. The pharaohs of this amazing civilization, known for its impressive pyramids and breathtaking temples, held absolute authority for long periods of time. King Khufu of Egypt was one of the most important people in history because he ordered the building of the Great Pyramid of Giza, one of the Seven Wonders of the Ancient World. The pyramid is a testament to the outstanding capabilities and organisational abilities of ancient Egyptians, who used cutting-edge engineering and architectural techniques in its creation.

The Nile River was crucial to Egypt's prosperity and stability because it allowed for increased agricultural production and commerce. Egypt was able to prosper and survive for millennia thanks to the Nile's periodic flooding, which offered good soil for agriculture.

Thinkers and Philosophers of Ancient Greece's Golden Age

The intellectual awakening that the ancient Greeks initiated was crucial to the development of Western culture. Socrates, Plato, and Aristotle are often cited as pivotal figures in the history of philosophy and critical thought. The method of inquiry that Socrates developed, known as Socratic dialogue, is still widely used today.

One of the earliest recorded institutions of higher learning was established by Plato, a disciple of Socrates, at the Academy in Athens. A lot of his philosophical writings, especially "The Republic," dealt with questions of social justice, government, and the perfect community. Aristotle was Plato's most renowned student, and he went on to make significant contributions to philosophy, biology, politics, and ethics. His writings were seminal for the development of the scientific method and had an impact on many academics who came after him.

The Romans paved the way for civilization and codified the law.

The Roman Empire is widely regarded as one of the greatest civilizations ever due to its extensive territorial expansion and long-lasting impact on government and the law. Caesar, Augustus, and Cicero were among the empire's most influential leaders.

Thanks to his brilliance as a general and a statesman, Julius Caesar brought an end to the Roman Republic and cleared the way for the Roman Empire. His death on the Ides of March in 44 BCE was a watershed moment in Roman history, ushering in the reign of Augustus, his grandnephew and adopted son. Augustus instituted extensive reforms that ensured the continued success of the Roman Empire.

The great Roman statesman, orator, and philosopher Cicero advocated for democratic rule and the rule of law. His political philosophy publications and lectures are still read and respected today.

The Renaissance saw a creative and intellectual renaissance.

Art, science, and humanism all flourished throughout the Renaissance, a cultural and intellectual movement that took place in Europe from the 14th to the 17th centuries. Leonardo da Vinci, Michelangelo, and Galileo Galilei are just a few of the iconic figures who exemplified this revolutionary time in history.

Leonardo da Vinci was a Renaissance polymath who mastered many disciplines. He was a master artist, sculptor, anatomist, engineer, and mathematician. His most famous paintings, "Mona Lisa" and "The Last Supper," are universally regarded as artistic high points.

Another Renaissance giant, Michelangelo is most known for his spectacular frescoes on the Sistine Chapel ceiling and sculptures like "David" and "The Pieta," which have become iconic works of art. When it comes to depicting the human body, no one can match his skill or depth of feeling.

Galileo Galilei, an early scientist, argued that the heliocentric model of the universe was more accurate than the then-common geocentric one. His telescopic studies of objects in space, including as Jupiter's moons and Venus's phases, ushered in a new era of cosmic comprehension.

Globalisation and Technological Advancement in Today's World

Even as we enter the modern period, influential people and cultures have been moulding our globalised society. The advances in manufacturing, transportation, and communication that sparked Britain's Industrial Revolution in the late 18th century triggered widespread social upheaval.

James Watt, who perfected the steam engine, and Thomas Edison, who invented the electric light bulb and phonograph, are two examples of the pioneering thinkers who propelled the Industrial Revolution forward. Their work ushered in the era of mass production and technological advancement.

Superpowers like the United States and the Soviet Union emerged in the twentieth century, each with their own sphere of influence and ideology. The outcome of World War II and the postwar international order were significantly influenced by the likes of Franklin D. Roosevelt and Winston Churchill.

Culture, business, and communication were all impacted by the rise of digital technology in the late 20th and early 21st centuries. The Internet was pioneered by Tim Berners-Lee, who expanded people's access to information and communication, and by Steve Jobs, co-founder of Apple Inc., who revolutionised personal computing, music, and telephony.

In sum, human history is a rich tapestry.

Numerous influential people and cultures contributed to the fabric that is human history. Key figures and civilizations have left behind a rich legacy, from Mesopotamia's cradle of civilization to ancient Egypt's zenith to Greece's intellectual enlightenment to the Roman Empire's opulence to the Renaissance's cultural rebirth to the modern era's globalisation and innovation.

Their impact can be seen throughout disciplines, from philosophy and law to the arts, sciences, and technologies. They have influenced how we think, rule, create, and communicate. It is important, as we continue to deal with the difficulties of the modern world, to think about the important people and cultures that have influenced our development.

Chapter 4.
Silk and spices: Silk Road wares

4.1- In-depth examination of the various goods traded along the route

The Silk Road was a network of trade routes that connected Asia, the Middle East, and even some of Europe. It was more than just a way to get products from one place to another; it was also a way for people to communicate and share ideas. It woven a complex web of trade that connected the far reaches of the globe with commodities both familiar and unusual. In this investigation, we will uncover the jewels and commodities that fed this ancient trading network by taking a close look at the wide variety of items that circulated over the Silk Road.

Silk: The Most Desired Good

Silk, the most valuable and most sought after commodity trafficked on the Silk Road, gives the road its name. For decades, the Chinese essentially controlled the market for this expensive fabric by guarding their silk production secret. Silk was so highly prized by the Roman Empire's upper class that it was shipped west along the Silk Road.

Silk was more than just a status symbol; its light weight and breathability made it an ideal fabric for clothes. Silk was so highly sought after in the West that it was eventually used as currency all along the trade route known as the Silk Road. Silk was a common medium of transaction among merchants and was crucial to the Silk Road's thriving economy.

Treasures of Flavorful Scents

Another valuable item traded on the Silk Road was spices. Exotic spices like cinnamon, pepper, nutmeg, and cloves were in high demand due to their culinary, medicinal, and preservation functions. Spices were utilised in cooking, medicine, cosmetics, fragrances, and incense, among other things.

The Spice Islands of Southeast Asia and the Indian subcontinent are the places of origin for many of these spices. Along the Silk Road, they were introduced to the Mediterranean and Europe, where they quickly became staples in cooking and helped spur the creation of regionally distinct recipes.

Gold, silver, and gems all serve as status symbols

Along the Silk Road, the most valuable goods were gold, silver, and precious stones. In addition to its decorative and ornamentation functions, precious metals and gems served as currency and were held as valuable assets. Crowns, jewellery, and religious artefacts from nations all along the Silk Road frequently featured these symbols of riches and power.

Due to its abundance of gold and gemstones, India was an important player in the global trade of these goods. Gold and diamonds from India were traded with Western civilizations, notably the Roman Empire, thanks to the Silk Road.

Cultural Diversity in Textiles and Carpets

The Silk Road's trade relied heavily on textiles and carpets, which displayed the diverse nations' rich artistic and artisanal heritages. In particular, carpets rose in popularity, with Persian rugs becoming known for their beauty and quality around the world.

China, Iran, and Central Asia were all well-known for their textile industries, and the Silk Road facilitated the export of their wares to other parts of the world. These fabrics frequently displayed intricate patterns and motifs that drew inspiration from local traditions.

Chinese Treasures: Tea and Porcelain

Both tea and porcelain, two iconic Chinese exports, travelled far and wide on the Silk Road. Green tea from China, in particular, spread throughout Central Asia and beyond. In addition to its refreshing flavour, people appreciated it for the health benefits it provided and the part it played in cultural ceremonies.

The exquisite beauty and practicality of porcelain—or "china" as it was known in the West—made in China, was highly valued. The elaborate patterns and vivid colours used to make Chinese porcelain became a status symbol in many countries.

The Intellectual Currency of Paper and Printing

Trade in physical items such as silk, spices, and precious metals was the Silk Road's bread and butter, but the flow of ideas and information was just as important. Along the Silk Road, the spread of information was revolutionised by the Chinese development of papermaking and woodblock printing.

The invention of paper facilitated the dissemination of knowledge, literature, and sacred texts because it was a portable and inexpensive medium for doing so. The dissemination of Buddhist scriptures in particular via these routes aided in the eventual expansion of Buddhism throughout Asia.

Traditional Use of Medicinal Plants and Other Healing Modalities

Herbal cures and other forms of traditional medicine were a major commodity on the Silk Road. Along the way, many different societies traded medicinal knowledge and ingredients with one another, often utilising local botanicals and healing methods.

Particularly significant was the ancient and comprehensive pharmacopoeia of Chinese herbal therapy. The healing powers of herbs like ginseng and rhubarb made them desirable in both Eastern and Western medicine. Along the Silk Road, these herbs were essential for treating illness and sustaining good health.

The Silk Road relied on horses and other livestock for transportation.

Livestock and other animals were also traded along the Silk Road. Particularly important to the Silk Road economy were horses. In exchange for other things, the Chinese, who are well-known for their expertise in horse breeding, supplied numerous empires and kingdoms with high-quality war horses.

Another important mode of transportation along the Silk Road were camels, which are well-suited to the desert climate. They were able to travel long distances and carry huge goods over the rough terrain of Central Asia. The use of camels on the Silk Road resulted in the famed "camel caravans" that travelled its length.

A Woven Web of International Commerce and Cultural Exchange

The Silk Road was an active medium for the diffusion of information, as well as the exchange of ideas and products. The economic growth and cultural diversity that resulted from the trade of silk, spices, precious metals, textiles, tea, and porcelain throughout its length cannot be overstated. The Silk Road promoted communication between northern and southern regions and helped people of different faiths and ethnicities learn from and adapt to one another. Its history continues to shape our globalised world today, and it serves as a tribute to the human urge for exploration, trade, and cultural exchange.

4.2- Their cultural, economic, and social impact

Cultures, economies, and communities all along the Silk Road, a network of trade routes connecting Asia, the Middle East, and parts of Europe, were profoundly and irrevocably impacted. This ancient trading system connected more than just buyers and sellers; it also allowed for the dissemination of new ideas, innovations, and worldviews. The Silk Road had profound effects on society, economy, and culture, and we'll examine all three here to learn more about how it moulded the past.

Cultural Effects: How Ideas and Values Travel the World

As people from all parts of the world travelled from East to West along the Silk Road, they brought with them their own unique customs, beliefs, and artistic manifestations, creating a bustling corridor of cultural exchange.

One of the Silk Road's most profound cultural effects was the spread of religions. Along the Silk Road, Buddhism spread from India through Central Asia, China, and beyond. Similarly, Islam, which originated in the Arabian Peninsula, eventually made its way to Central Asia and even China. Syncretism, the merging of multiple belief systems, led to the development of new religious practises and traditions as a result of the dissemination of religious concepts.

Various cultural aesthetics and artistic traditions were influenced by the Silk Road's promotion of the exchange of art and craftsmanship. Persian carpets and decorative motifs made their way into Central Asian and Chinese art, and vice versa for Chinese silk, porcelain, and calligraphy. Along the Silk Road, artists and craftspeople were able to share knowledge and materials, leading to the development of innovative new styles.

The trading routes served as a channel for the dissemination of literary and linguistic traditions. Lingua Franca, a commercial language, was developed as a result of the widespread multilingualism of merchants and travellers. Religious books, philosophical treatises, and historical chronicles were all translated and widely disseminated, resulting in a fertile environment for the exchange of ideas and information.

The Silk Road was instrumental in the spread of new ideas and innovations in science and technology. Technology from China was sent to the West, where it influenced other regions. This included the spread of papermaking, printing, and gunpowder to places like the Middle East and Europe. On the other hand, China benefited from the spread of Western science and philosophy from ancient Greece and Rome.

Implications for Trade and Economic Growth

Trade, new opportunities for making money, and overall economic growth were all boosted by the Silk Road's connectivity.

The Silk Road's principal function was to promote the exchange of expensive luxury goods. Silk, spices, gold, jewels, and exotic fabrics were among the most sought after items. The producers in the East and the buyers in the West both benefited from this luxury goods trade, which boosted economies all the way around.

The Silk Road allowed for the creation of complex monetary and banking institutions. Money was exchanged using a wide variety of coins and paper bills. Banks and credit systems were developed by merchants to aid in international trade. Large-scale trade caravans wouldn't have been possible without these financial breakthroughs, which also served to stabilise economies.

The Silk Road's economic impact was seen in many ways than only the trade of commodities, though. Industries producing literature, art, and music flourished as a result of increased cultural interchange. The creative works produced along the trade routes not only functioned as important commodities, but also boosted the cultural and economic vitality of the communities involved.

The Silk Road was a fertile environment for new ideas and business ventures. To satisfy the needs of faraway consumers, merchants and craftspeople invented cutting-edge tools and production techniques. Caravanserais, oasis, and well-organized trade routes were all products of this enterprising mentality.

Impact on Society: Cultural Mixing and Societies of Variation

The Silk Road influenced the development of the nations it passed through, producing multiethnic communities with intricate webs of shared history and culture.

The trade routes fostered a cosmopolitan society by connecting people of many nationalities, languages, and cultures. Urban centres along the Silk Road encouraged cultural diversity and cosmopolitanism. Because of this variety, tolerance and mutual respect flourished among these groups.

Urbanisation: The economic expansion spurred by Silk Road trade fueled the development of large cities. Samarkand, Bukhara, and Xi'an, among others, thrived as economic, cultural, and intellectual centres. Improvements in building design, public works, and administrative frameworks are just some of the outcomes of urbanisation.

The Silk Road allowed people to rise in their own social classes. Through trade, people from many walks of life might rise to positions of power and prosperity. This ascent challenged established social and economic order, giving people more say over their lives and opportunities.

Cultural mingling occurred as a result of contacts made by travellers on the Silk Road. The merging of Eastern and Western ideas resulted in the creation of novel customs, cuisines, and aesthetic movements. The people who lived near these roads saw great benefits from this cultural mixing.

Final Thoughts: A Lasting Impact

The Silk Road was more than just a network of commerce routes; it also served as a vehicle for the transmission of ideas, beliefs, and cultures between the various civilizations it linked. Religions, creative styles, and scientific ideas all travelled farther and faster as a result of it. The economy benefited from the free flow of high-end commodities, the introduction of new banking techniques, and the development of creative fields. In terms of society, it ushered in more tolerant and mobile communities rich with cultural diversity.

Globalisation has continued the Silk Road's legacy of easing the flow of products, ideas, and civilizations across borders. Because of the Silk Road, people from all walks of life have been inspired to forge connections across cultures and continents in an effort to better understand one another.

Chapter 5.
Cultural and Religious Globalisation

5.1- How the Silk Road facilitated the exchange of ideas, religions, and philosophies

The Silk Road connected Asia, the Middle East, and some regions of Europe through a complex network of trade routes that served as a meeting place for people of many different cultures and beliefs. This ancient trade route connected people from all walks of life and throughout the globe and through the ages, fostering a profound exchange of ideas and spiritual values. In this investigation, we will dive into the role that the Silk Road played in the interchange of ideas, the proliferation of faiths, and the development of ideologies.

Cultures met and clashed along the Silk Road.

The Silk Road was more than a commercial thoroughfare; it was also a meeting place for people of varying ethnicities, linguistic groups, and religious persuasions. The meeting of so many different cultures made for fruitful dialogue.

Linguistic Exchange: Many Silk Road traders, tourists, and ambassadors spoke more than one language. Because of the variety of languages spoken, it was easier for people to interact and share ideas. The ability of translators to communicate across cultural boundaries was critical in the development of humankind.

Cultural Fusion: The Silk Road fostered interaction between people of different backgrounds. People from diverse areas began exchanging cultural practises like music, painting, and cooking. As a result of this mixing of cultures, novel and original ways of expressing thought and feeling emerged.

The role of the Silk Road in the proliferation of religions.

The Silk Road was instrumental in the dissemination of various religious tenets and practises. It was a means via which many different religions, including Buddhism, Islam, Christianity, Zoroastrianism, and Manichaeism, spread over the world.

Buddhism is one of the most visible manifestations of religious exchange along the Silk Road. Buddhism was born in India and has since expanded across the rest of Asia, particularly China and Southeast Asia. The trade routes aided in the dissemination of Buddhist scholars, texts, and artefacts, which in turn aided in the development of Buddhist settlements and the building of monasteries.

Islam: originating in the Arabian Peninsula, Islam travelled along the Silk Road to reach the rest of the world. The dissemination of Islamic ideas and culture was greatly aided by Muslim merchants and academics. Central Asian cities like Samarkand and Bukhara benefited from their Silk Road location by becoming major hubs of Islamic learning and culture.

Christianity: Christianity spread eastward via the paths of international trade. Communities and churches belonging to the Eastern Christian sect known as Nestorianism can be found in places as diverse as Persia, Central Asia, and even China. These groups facilitated communication between different faiths and helped spread new ideas.

Manichaeism, a syncretic faith founded by Mani, and Zoroastrianism, an ancient religion of Persia, both travelled down the Silk Road. Central Asia and beyond became home to followers of both faiths, enriching the region's religious variety.

Thoughts and Ideas Swapped Along the Silk Road

Although its primary function was the spread of religion, the Silk Road also served as a conduit for the interchange of philosophical ideas. Meeting and influencing one another, philosophers, academics, and thinkers from diverse cultures came together.

Hellenistic thinking, which originated in the philosophical canon of ancient Greece, spread to the far reaches of the Silk Road's eastern reaches. Scholars from all over the world, from Central Asia to the Far East, translated and studied Greek classics, including the works of thinkers like Aristotle, Plato, and Epicurus. Syncretic schools of thought emerged as a result of the merging of Greek concepts and Eastern philosophies.

Chinese Philosophy: The Silk Road served as a vehicle for the dissemination of Confucianism, Daoism, and Legalism from China to other parts of Asia and the world. The cultural and religious beliefs of the areas they spread to were shaped by these philosophical schools.

During the Islamic Golden Age, Muslim philosophers and scholars met and discussed ideas with their peers from other cultures, laying the groundwork for what is now known as Islamic Philosophy. Because of this intellectual boom, many ancient Greek, Persian, and Indian books were eventually translated into Arabic and used to inform the growth of Islamic philosophy and the dissemination of information along the Silk Road.

Syncretism and Cultural Encounters

Cultural exchanges and syncretism, the fusing of different traditions to create something new, occurred frequently along the Silk Road because of its diverse population.

Artistic Syncretism: the emergence of new forms of art that reflect the blending of civilizations as a result of the sharing of artistic styles and techniques. For instance, the fusion of Chinese and Persian decorative art elements resulted in a new and original style.

There was also a blending of architectural motifs and styles. Central Asian Buddhist stupas, for example, incorporated elements of Persian architecture into their designs, creating a hybrid style that reflected the contributions of both cultures.

Culinary Exchange: The sharing of ingredients and methods of preparation has improved culinary cultures around the world. Regional foods and spices travelled to other areas, inspiring exciting new culinary traditions.

Summing Up: A Woven Web of Concepts and Values

Culturally rich and laced with commercial channels, the Silk Road was a dynamic channel for the dissemination of new ideas, philosophies, and faiths. It helped spread not only major world religions like Buddhism, Islam, and Christianity, but also philosophical and intellectual ideas from one culture to another. Beyond the tangible wealth it generated, the Silk Road also had a lasting imprint on our modern, linked world by weaving together a complex tapestry of beliefs, ideas, and cultural expressions.

5.2- Notable thinkers and religious figures associated with the route

In addition to facilitating the movement of goods between East and West, the Silk Road also functioned as a channel for the dissemination of new ideas, ideologies, and religious beliefs. Over the course of its long existence, this ancient network witnessed the passage of countless great philosophers and religious leaders whose ideas and teachings left permanent imprints on the nations they visited. In this investigation, we will look into the lives of some influential individuals connected to the Silk Road.

Buddha is the Awakened One.

The Buddha, or Siddhartha Gautama, is a major character in the history of the Silk Road. He was a prince in what is now Nepal, but he gave it all up to find the source of all pain and enlightenment in the sixth century BCE. The Buddha spent the remainder of his life educating others after he attained enlightenment under the Bodhi tree.

His teachings eventually gave rise to Buddhism, one of the most widely practised religions in the Silk Road region. Long voyages were undertaken by Buddhist monks and missionaries along these trade routes, bearing with them not only the teachings of the Buddha but also Buddhist art and architecture. Numerous Buddhist temples, stupas, and works of art testify to Buddhism's far-reaching influence on the aesthetics and practises of the Silk Road's many communities.

Pathfinder of the Silk Road, Zhang Qian

Zhang Qian wasn't a philosopher or religious leader, yet his travels along the Silk Road changed the course of commerce and cultural interchange for centuries. Zhang Qian, a 2nd-century BCE Chinese explorer and diplomat, is commonly referred to as the "Father of the

Silk Road." The eastern Mediterranean was the westernmost point of his journeys into Central Asia.

Zhang Qian's journeys paved the way for new commercial routes and strengthened diplomatic ties between the Han Dynasty in China and the kingdoms of Central Asia. His writings about the places he saw popularised the Silk Road and encouraged subsequent explorers, merchants, and religious leaders to use it.

The Journey of Xuanzang, Scholar

During the seventh century CE, the Chinese Buddhist monk and scholar Xuanzang, also known as Hsüan-tsang, set off on a journey of a lifetime to India. His principal objective was to amass Buddhist holy scriptures and expand his knowledge of Buddhist thought. His travels along the Silk Road took him across cultures and perilous landscapes.

In addition to his religious goals, Xuanzang's travels were an academic adventure. His goal was to return canonical Buddhist texts to China, where different views of Buddhism had led to confusion. As a result of his efforts, many Buddhist writings were translated into Chinese, allowing for a deeper knowledge of Buddhist theory and philosophy in that country.

Xuanzang returned to China and had a significant impact on Chinese Buddhism, as well as the country's spiritual and philosophical environment, through his writings and lectures. His writings about the places he visited along the Silk Road are now considered vital historical documents.

The Venetian Explorer Marco Polo

The Venetian merchant and traveller Marco Polo is another well-known character connected to the Silk Road. During the 13th century, Polo travelled to China with his family to visit the Mongol emperor Kublai Khan. Along the Silk Road, they experienced new civilizations and were exposed to the incredible wealth and splendour of the Far East.

After returning to Europe, Marco Polo wrote about his adventures in "The Travels of Marco Polo," which spurred widespread interest in the Silk Road's wealth. Despite initial scepticism, his writings came to be relied upon as authoritative accounts of the countries and peoples of the East.

Islamic Traveller Ibn Battuta

In the 14th century, the Moroccan explorer and scholar Ibn Battuta set out on an extraordinary voyage that would take him all the way along the Silk Road and beyond. His initial inspiration for setting out on this adventure was to make the Islamic pilgrimage to the holy city of Mecca. But his restless spirit compelled him to see the world, and he ended up becoming one of the most well-traveled people in history.

The regions along the Silk Road that Ibn Battuta explored—Central Asia, India, and China—are rich in culture and tradition, and I learned a lot from reading Ibn Battuta's tales of his travels. His writings are not just a record of the cultural diversity he encountered along the Silk Road, but also of his own spiritual and intellectual development.

Mara Bar Seraphim: A Syrian Philosopher

A Syrian philosopher and writer named Mara Bar-Serapion lived in the second century CE and is one of the Silk Road's lesser-known figures. His works shed light on the intellectual interactions that took place along these ancient trade routes, and while his name may not be as well-known as some of the others named, they are no less insightful for that.

One of the most influential works of Mara Bar-Serapion is a letter he sent to his son while incarcerated; in it, he discusses the collapse and resurgence of empires and the lasting influence of thinkers like Socrates, Pythagoras, and the Jewish prophets. The pursuit of knowledge, wisdom, and ethics were all topics he broached in his philosophical reflections. Although he was not a religious leader, his works are illustrative of the concepts that were shared between cultures because to the Silk Road.

Conclusion: A Rich Web of Intercultural Contact

Cultural interaction and intellectual development flourished along the Silk Road's extensive network of trade routes spanning thousands of kilometres. Famous intellectuals, religious leaders, explorers, and thinkers all travelled its length, enriching the fabric of ideas, beliefs, and philosophies that inform our modern perspective. The legacy of enlightenment, spiritual awakening, and intellectual curiosity left by these individuals connected people from all walks of life along the Silk Road.

Chapter 6.
The Mighty Empires of the Silk Road

6.1- Exploration of the empires that controlled portions of the Silk Road

Over the course of its long history, the Silk Road, a network of trade routes connecting Asia, the Middle East, and some regions of Europe, saw the birth and fall of many great civilizations. These empires were instrumental in defining the areas the Silk Road traversed. In this investigation, we will examine the contributions, legacies, and effects of some of the most powerful dynasties that ruled over sections of the Silk Road.

The Persian Empire: An Essential Cog in World Trade

The Achaemenid and Sassanian periods of the Persian Empire were among the earliest and most influential in terms of their control over the Silk Road. The Persian Empire served as an important crossroads for East-West trade and cultural exchange because of its central location.

The Persian Royal Road was built by the Achaemenid Empire (550-330 BCE) to link Persia and Anatolia (present-day Turkey). The swift transport of commodities and communications across the huge empire was made possible by this road. Merchants and travellers felt more secure because of the efforts of Persian administrators to establish and maintain order along the trade routes.

The successor empire to the Achaemenids, the Sassanian Empire (ca. 224-651 CE), saw the Silk Road flourish. The participation of Persian merchants and artisans in commerce along these routes facilitated the movement of high-end consumer items, artistic techniques, and cultural ideas between the East and the West. The strategic position of the Sasanian Empire along the Silk Road encouraged multiculturalism and the free flow of ideas.

A Trading Hub at the Western Edge of the Roman Empire

From the first century BCE through the fifth century CE, when the Roman Empire was at its height, it governed the western end of the Silk Road. Trade with the East was driven by the Roman need for luxury items like silk, spices, and precious metals. In the Han Dynasty of China, the great Silk Road explorer Zhang Qian met Roman traders in Central Asia.

It was common practise for Roman traders to venture through the rival Parthian Empire and into Central Asia in search of unusual things to buy with their gold and silver. The exchange of goods and ideas between Romans and Asians through trade had far-reaching effects on both cultures.

A Roman Challenger: The Parthian Empire

From the third century BCE until the third century CE, the Parthian Empire, a great Iranian empire, dominated the area of the Silk Road that is now modern-day Iran and Iraq. The Parthians' elite cavalry and command of important trade routes earned them widespread respect.

The Parthians were instrumental in establishing trade routes between Asia and Europe. They worked as go-betweens for trade between the Roman Empire and Asian countries like China and India. Ctesiphon, the Parthian capital, flourished as a commercial and cultural hub.

The Eastern Trade Gateway in the Han Dynasty

China's Han Dynasty (206 BCE-220 CE) was pivotal to the Silk Road's eastern end. Chinese silk, a much-coveted luxury product, was shipped over these routes in large quantities. The Han Dynasty ensured a steady supply of high-quality silk for commerce by establishing a government monopoly on silk production.

Famous Chinese explorer Zhang Qian was among the merchants and diplomats who travelled westward to forge relationships with regional powers in Central Asia and the Middle East. The spread of commerce and cultural interactions was aided by Zhang Qian's writings about his trips along the Silk Road.

5. The Tang Dynasty, the Silk Road's Golden Age

Many historians believe that the Silk Road's heyday occurred during the Tang Dynasty (618-907 CE) in China. China's economy, culture, and Silk Road trade all flourished to new heights during this time.

Tang Dynasty Emperor Taizong was an advocate for diplomatic and economic ties to kingdoms in Central Asia and the Middle East. The Tang capital of Chang'an (modern Xi'an) grew into a cosmopolitan centre that attracted travellers from all over the world. The spread of Buddhism was aided by pilgrims like Xuanzang who travelled west along the Silk Road in pursuit of holy writings in India.

Because of the Tang Dynasty's rule, trade, ideas, and religion were all free to travel over the eastern section of the Silk Road. Along the trading routes, Chinese silk, ceramics, tea, and paper items were in high demand. The cultural and social landscapes of Central Asia and the Middle East were profoundly impacted by the Tang Dynasty.

The Mongols, Step #6: Integrating the Silk Road

In the 13th and 14th centuries, the Mongol Empire, led by Genghis Khan and his successors, established one of the world's largest territorial conquests. Their hegemony covered most of the Silk Road, from China to Europe.

The Mongols encouraged commerce and cultural interaction throughout their enormous territories. Marco Polo, a famous traveller from Venice, documented his journey along the Silk Road, which he took through lands ruled by the Mongols. The Pax Mongolica (Mongol Peace) made it easier for traders to move goods over the Silk Road without fear of attack.

The Mongol Empire acted as a bridge between the East and the West, allowing for the dissemination of new ideas and cultural practises. Western cultures adopted Chinese innovations like gunpowder, papermaking, and printing, while Eastern cultures adopted European ones like astronomy and mathematics.

The Last Word: Silk Road Superpowers

The cultural, commercial, and intercultural contacts between people of different backgrounds left by the Silk Road dynasties are being felt today. Important stretches of the Silk Road were under these empires' authority, allowing for the freer exchange of commerce and ideas between East and West. Our modern, interconnected world continues to draw inspiration from the Silk Road dynasties' contributions to history, trade, and culture.

6.2- The rise and fall of these empires

The development and collapse of great empires that ruled over different parts of the Silk Road is as much a part of its history as the flow of products, ideas, and cultures from one place to another. Trade routes, cultural interactions, and the fundamental fabric of society were all profoundly impacted by the dominance of these empires. In this investigation, we will take a close look at the growth and fall of some major Silk Road-related dynasties.

1. The Rise of the Persian Empire

Rise: An important turning point in Silk Road history occurred with the emergence of the Persian Empire, especially during the Achaemenid period (c. 550-330 BCE). Cyrus the Great oversaw the fast expansion of the Persian Empire, which included the conquest of large portions of the Near Eastern regions of Anatolia, Mesopotamia, and Egypt.

The Achaemenid kings, most especially Darius I, understood the significance of the Silk Road as a conduit for commerce between Asia and Europe. Trade was made easier and safer as a result of their establishment of a standardised currency and the famous Royal Road, a large network of highways.

Fall: Alexander the Great's conquests in the fourth century BCE eventually brought down the Achaemenid Empire. There is still evidence of the Persian Empire's influence on the Silk Road today, thanks to its promotion of commerce and cultural interaction.

The Roman Empire was the doorway to the Western world.

Rise: From the first century BCE to the fifth century CE, the Roman Empire controlled much of the known world from its western border on the Silk Road. The advent of Rome and her subsequent conquest of the Mediterranean and beyond ushered in a golden age of commerce and economic growth.

The Romans' insatiable appetite for Eastern curios fueled a booming trade along the Silk Road. In order to gain access to important goods, they forged diplomatic links with multiple empires, especially the Parthians.

Fall: The decline of the Roman Empire was a slow process caused by internal strife, economic difficulties, and external aggressors. Western Roman Empire disintegrated in the fifth century CE due to a combination of external barbarian invasions and internal turmoil. The Eastern Roman Empire, or Byzantine Empire, persisted, however, for many more decades.

Third, the Parthian Empire—Rome's Rivals

Rise: In the third century BCE, the region was shaken by the rise of the Parthian Empire, which had its heart in the territory that is now Iran and Iraq. Because of its dominance in the Near East and other strategic locations along the Silk Road, it played a pivotal role in the flow of goods and ideas.

The Parthians were pivotal in the Silk Road's establishment because of their role as middlemen between the Roman Empire and the East. They helped bring these two civilizations closer together by facilitating trade and cultural exchange.

Fall: Internal strife and pressure from the Sasanian Empire to the east and Rome to the west contributed to the collapse and demise of the Parthian Empire in the third century CE. A change in regional dominance occurred with the rise of the Sassanians.

Eastern Trade Gateway in the Han Dynasty

Rise: The eastern end of the Silk Road was established during the Han Dynasty in China (206 BCE-220 CE). The Han Dynasty grew in size and influence under Emperor Wu, opening up trade routes to Central Asia and beyond.

The Han Dynasty actively encouraged its subjects to engage in commercial and diplomatic exchanges with their neighbours. The famed Chinese explorer Zhang Qian led a group of merchants and diplomats westward, paving the way for increased trade and cultural interchange between China and the rest of the world.

Fall: The internal warfare, economic difficulties, and political fragmentation that plagued the Han Dynasty in the third century CE contributed to its eventual demise. After the Han Dynasty collapsed, China went through a period of political instability and division known as the Three Kingdoms era.

5. The Golden Age of the Tang Dynasty

Rise: Many historians believe that the Silk Road's heyday occurred during the Tang Dynasty (618-907 CE). Along the routes of commerce, the sphere of influence and economic and cultural activity of China grew.

The Tang Dynasty, led by Emperor Taizong, encouraged commerce with Central Asia and the Middle East. Merchants, diplomats, and scholars from all over the world flocked to Chang'an (modern Xi'an), the capital city.

Fall: Political instability, economic difficulties, and outside threats all contributed to the Tang Dynasty's fall in the 9th century CE. The sheer size of the empire made it a nightmare to administer, and it eventually collapsed under the weight of both internal and external threats.

Pax Mongolica (No. 6) — The Mongol Empire

Rise: Genghis Khan and his descendants led the Mongol Empire to greatness in the 13th and 14th centuries. One of the largest land empires in history was founded as a result of its conquests.

The Silk Road was made safer by the Mongols, who encouraged trade and cultural interaction across their enormous territories. During the Pax Mongolica, a period of relative calm, trade and cultural interaction flourished.

Fall: Internal struggle and the subsequent breakup of the Mongol Empire into separate Khanates contributed significantly to the empire's demise. By the end of the 14th century, the Mongol Empire was much smaller and weaker than it had been.

Finishing: The Lasting Impression

History's ebb and flow, marked by conquests, trade, and cultural exchange, can be seen in the rise and fall of empires along the Silk Road. Although these empires have fallen and been forgotten, their cultural contributions, scientific advances, and the Silk Road itself live on. Stories of merchants, explorers, and intellectuals who travelled these ancient trade routes preserve the legacy of these empires for future generations.

Chapter 7.
The heyday of the Silk Road

7.1- Discussion of the peak of Silk Road trade and cultural exchange

When the ancient world was remarkably interwoven by a network of trade routes reaching from China to the Mediterranean, it was during the heyday of Silk Road trade and cultural exchange. Over the course of several centuries, the Silk Road flourished into a rich tapestry of diverse cultures, ideas, and civilizations, becoming much more than a simple trade route. This investigation will look into the causes of the Silk Road's commercial and cultural zenith, its central figures, and its long-lasting effects.

Reasons behind Silk Road Trade's Prosperity

The zenith of Silk Road commerce was made possible by a confluence of economic forces, including:

One, the need for Western luxury items fueled trade along the Silk Road. Silk, pearls, spices, and other exotic Chinese imports were greatly sought after in Western markets like Rome's. Want for these rare commodities pushed merchandise down the trading routes.

Second, Geographical Advantage: The Roman Empire, the Persian Empire, and the Tang Dynasty in China all benefited greatly from their respective locations. These states ruled important stretches of the Silk Road, which they used to promote trade and guarantee the safety of travellers.

Technology advancements, such as the camel saddle and better ship designs, facilitated faster travel along the Silk Road. Because of the increased capacity of caravans and ships, trading became more profitable.

4. Monetary Systems: The adoption of a unified monetary system, as shown with the introduction of the Roman denarius and the Chinese cash coin, simplified commerce and increased its accessibility.

5. Political Stability: Interactions between nations were less likely to be disrupted by war during times of political calm, such as the Pax Romana in the Roman Empire and the Pax Mongolica in the Mongol Empire.

The Silk Road as a Route for Cultural Contact

The Silk Road served as a platform for the interchange of not only goods but also ideas, philosophies, and even political systems. This fruitful mingling of cultures was facilitated by a number of factors:

Major cities along the Silk Road, including as Chang'an, Samarkand, and Constantinople, acted as cultural crossroads and became hubs of diversity. These cities were melting pots where people of all walks of life, languages, and faiths could come together. Because of this variety, cultural influences were able to mix and mingle.

Second, Religious Diffusion: The Silk Road was crucial to the dissemination of faiths. Buddhism, for instance, spread from India to the rest of Asia via these commercial routes, making its way to China and Southeast Asia. Similarly to how Christianity made its way eastward over the Silk Road, Islam expanded across Central Asia and into China.

Thirdly, throughout the Silk Road, artists and craftspeople shared ideas, inspiration, and even finished products with one another. As a result of this interaction between the creative communities of East and West, new and exciting styles of art and architecture emerged.

The translation of works of literature and intellectual treatises promoted the dissemination of information and new ideas. Philosophical and scientific works from ancient Greece, India, and China were translated into many languages.

Fifthly, the Diffusion of Technologies and Innovations was aided by the Silk Road. Western civilization was impacted by Chinese innovations such as papermaking, printing, and gunpowder since they were exported to the West. On the other hand, China benefited from the spread of Greek and Roman scientific and philosophical ideas.

Influential Participants in Silk Road-Related Commercial and Cultural Exchange

Trade and cultural interchange were greatly advanced by the efforts of Chinese merchants, diplomats, and explorers. Xuanzang and Zhang Qian are only two historical figures who gained notoriety for their Silk Road travels.

Second, Roman merchants were enthusiastic buyers of Eastern wares like Chinese silk and Indian spices. The Silk Road wouldn't have been possible without their commerce with the East.

Important stretches of the Silk Road were governed by empires like the Parthian, Kushan, and Turkic Khaganate in Central Asia. Through their efforts, commercial and cultural exchanges between East and West were facilitated.

Fourth, the Mongol Empire: The Silk Road's heyday was during the Mongols' rule, specifically during the Pax Mongolica. Merchants and travellers were protected because of the Mongols' massive realm.

The Lasting Effects of the Silk Road's Commercial and Cultural Pinnacle

The world was profoundly and permanently altered by the zenith of Silk Road commerce and cultural exchange:

One example of globalisation is the Silk Road, which connected and affected many different cultures. This notion of interdependence paved the way for the spread of commerce and ideas over the world.

Papermaking and printing were just two examples of the technological developments that spread down the Silk Road and paved the way for the Renaissance in Europe and other parts of the world.

Third, Religious Influence: Buddhism, Islam, Christianity, and other religions' propagation along the Silk Road left an indelible mark on Eurasia's religious and cultural environment.

4. Art and Aesthetics: The distinctive forms of art, architecture, and craftsmanship that sprang from the artistic interchange along the Silk Road continue to inspire and influence modern design.

5. Cultural Syncretism: The Silk Road encouraged cultural syncretism, a phenomenon in which elements of diverse cultures mingled to create novel and exciting practises, foods, and art forms.

In conclusion, the zenith of Silk Road trade and cultural interchange was an unprecedented high point in the history of globalisation. It was a time when East and West grew more intertwined than ever before, and people from both regions began trading commodities and ideas with one another. Silk Road's legacy lives on, serving as a constant reminder of the world-changing power of cultural exchange and the limitless potential of human collaboration.

7.2- Cities and landmarks that thrived during this period

Numerous cities and landmarks rose to prominence as thriving hubs of Silk Road trade, culture, and intellectual interaction. These cities and landmarks were vital in historical development since they were important stops along the ancient Silk Road. Some of the most important cities and sites of this age of unprecedented global connectivity will be the focus of our investigation.

1. The Eastern Endpoint, Chang'an (Xi'an), China

Chang'an, now called Xi'an, served as the capital of the Han and Tang dynasties and as the eastern terminus of the Silk Road. During the height of Silk Road trade, it was one of the world's most populous and culturally diverse metropolises.

Trade: Chang'an was a major hub along the Silk Road where merchants came to buy, sell, and barter. Foreign traders provided spices, precious metals, and textiles, while Chinese silk, ceramics, and paper items were in high demand.

The city's population was made up of merchants, diplomats, and intellectuals from all over the world, which led to a rich environment for the interchange of ideas and cultural traditions. Ideas, faiths, and tongues all mingled together there.

The legendary journey to India by the Chinese Buddhist monk and traveller Xuanzang (sometimes spelled Hsüan-tsang) began at Chang'an. Along the Silk Road, he helped disseminate Buddhist teachings and facilitate the sharing of ideas.

The Terracotta Army, discovered not far from Xi'an, is a relic of China's ancient past and a UNESCO World Heritage site. The first

Chinese emperor, Qin Shi Huang, was buried with an army of life-size terracotta soldiers and horses to protect him in the afterlife.

The Uzbek capital of Samarkand has been called "the crossroads of cultures."

Modern-day Uzbekistan is home to the once-famous Central Asian city of Samarkand, which was an important stop along the Silk Road and a symbol of the region's opulence. Due to its advantageous position, it served as a hub for commercial and cultural interactions.

Samarkand served as the capital of the Timurid state, a prominent and strong Central Asian state, in the 14th and 15th centuries. The reign of Timur (Tamerlane) was a time of great cultural and architectural achievement for the city.

One of the most recognisable features of Samarkand is the Registan Square. It is bordered by three beautiful madrasas, or Islamic schools, each of which features ornate tilework and calligraphy. This public plaza was a hub for commerce and social activities.

Samarkand was also an important centre for scientific research and education. Ulugh Beg, a famous astronomer and mathematician, did much of his work at the Ulugh Beg Observatory, located in this city.

Thirdly, Kashgar, China, is known as the Silk Road's oasis.

Kashgar, in Xinjiang, China, was an important oasis city on the northern path of the Silk Road. Because of its convenient location on several major trade routes, it quickly grew into a thriving commercial hub.

Kashgar's bustling bazaars attracted buyers and sellers from all over Central Asia, Persia, and China, earning the city a reputation as a bustling marketplace. Rugs, clothes, spices, and even precious metals were all traded in the city.

The city's population of Uighurs, Persians, Mongols, and Chinese all brought something unique to the cultural pot. Kashgar was home to people of many different faiths and cultures.

Kashgar's well-preserved historic district, known as the "old town," is a great place to learn about the city's past and culture. With its winding lanes, mud-brick homes, and old-fashioned markets, it's like stepping back in time.

Palmyra, Syria: a Desert Paradise

Palmyra, in the Syrian desert, was an important stop for merchants and caravans on the western routes of the Silk Road. It was a vital halt for travellers because of its oasis setting in the desert.

Palmyra served as a key stop for caravans carrying goods between the Roman Empire and the Far East. It was crucial in easing business dealings between the two areas.

The city is well-known for its historical landmarks and architectural achievements, such as the Temple of Baalshamin and the Temple of Bel. These buildings are examples of a synthesis between classical Western and Eastern motifs.

Palmyra was a cultural crossroads where Eastern and Western influences mingled. The city's art, religion, and architecture reflected the mingling of many cultures.

5. Bukhara, Uzbekistan, Renowned for Its Academic Prowess

Located in what is now Uzbekistan, Bukhara was once a major stop along the Silk Road and a hub for education and culture. Many famous academics, scientists, and religious figures called it home.

The Bukhara School of Mathematics Mathematics and astronomy were two areas in which the city excelled. While based in Bukhara, scholars like as Al-Biruni and Al-Khwarizmi made substantial contributions to their respective professions.

There were a lot of caravanserais (roadside inns) in Bukhara for those on the Silk Road. These spots allowed for social interaction, commerce, and cultural sharing.

Bukhara was a hub for religious tolerance, with mosques, madrasas, and synagogues all operating side by side. It was a major hub for Islamic learning and Sufi mystical practise.

Sixth, the Rose-Red City of Petra in Jordan.

Located in the Jordanian desert, Petra was an important stop along the southern routes of the Silk Road in antiquity.

Petra was a major hub for commerce between Arabia, Egypt, and the Mediterranean. Its placement on major trade routes made it an ideal stop.

The Treasury (Al-Khazneh) and the Monastery (Ad Deir) are two of the most recognisable examples of the city's spectacular rock-cut architecture. These buildings are evidence of the ingenuity and skill of the people of Petra.

Among the many cultures with which the people of Petra traded were the Nabataeans, the Greeks, the Romans, and the Arabs. The city's buildings and artwork all show signs of this interaction.

Finally, we hear reverberations from the glorious past of the Silk Road.

During the height of Silk Road trade and cultural interchange, many cities and sites became bustling hubs of economic activity, artistic expression, and academic inquiry. They mirrored the ancient world's rich variety, inventiveness, and interdependence. Many of these cities have changed over time, but their histories live on as reminders of the Silk Road's illustrious past and of the human drive for knowledge, commerce, and cultural exchange.

Chapter 8.
Problems and Difficulties

8.1- Examination of the obstacles and dangers faced by Silk Road travelers

The Silk Road was a complex system of trade routes spanning thousands of kilometres, and its journeys were not for the faint of heart. Despite its importance in allowing for the spread of products, ideas, and cultures from one region to another, the Silk Road posed significant challenges to the brave adventurers who dared to travel it. In this investigation, we will look into the different challenges and dangers encountered by Silk Road travellers, illuminating the fortitude and ingenuity needed to traverse this ancient trading route.

Dangerous Ground, Part I: The Strenuous Physical Demands

From sweltering deserts to rocky mountains, the Silk Road went through it all. These geographical features presented substantial difficulties for travellers:

Huge deserts, such as the Taklamakan Desert in China and the Lut Desert in Iran, stood in the way of travellers along the Silk Road. Desert crossings were extremely dangerous due to the high heat, shifting sands, and lack of water.

Mountain Passes: Dangerous mountain passes were necessary to cross the Himalayas, Pamirs, and Tien Shan. Avalanches, precipitation, and steep inclines were only some of the challenges that tourists faced.

River Crossings: Obstacles included rivers such as the Amu Darya and the Indus. These rivers become extremely dangerous to cross during the spring thaw. The use of ferries, bridges, and even improvised rafts was commonplace.

2. Human Bandits and Raiders

Silk Road travellers regularly fretted about being attacked by humans. Remote and exposed regions were frequent targets for bandits and robbers waiting to pounce on unwary caravans.

Caravans were frequent targets of bandit attacks because of the wealth of commodities and currency they carried. To prevent or counter such attacks, travellers have to be alert and prepared.

Kidnappings for ransom were commonplace along the Silk Road. Abductions were most common among wealthy merchants and wealthy travellers.

Some bandit groups ran protection rackets, extorting money from caravans in exchange for letting them pass unmolested.

The Meteorological Challenges of Severe Weather

Travellers on the Silk Road had to deal with the unpredictable weather of the places through which it passed:

Travellers in the desert may be subjected to dangerous conditions due to sandstorms, which can limit visibility to near zero.

Suddenly occurring snowstorms in mountain passes could strand caravans and pose serious health hazards due to the extreme cold.

Heat and Dehydration: Travellers were at risk of heatstroke and dehydration while passing through desert regions.

4. Dangers to Health from Illness and Disease

Diseases and other health risks plagued those who travelled the Silk Road.

Malaria: Travellers risked catching malaria from insect bites in areas with stagnant water.

Water and food contamination can cause dysentery and other gastrointestinal diseases.

tiredness and Fatigue: Long journeys and their physical toll, coupled with exposure to harsh weather, frequently resulted in extreme tiredness and fatigue.

5. Difficulties in Communicating Due to Language and Cultural Differences

The Silk Road traversed a multilingual and multicultural area. This difference made it difficult for travellers to communicate:

The need for guides and interpreters who speak multiple languages was common in situations where participants spoke diverse languages.

Diplomacy and cultural awareness are vital abilities for travellers because of the potential for misunderstandings and disputes brought on by different cultural norms and practises.

Political Uncertainty: Global Issues #6

Several different countries and nomad groups could be encountered along the Silk Road. Trade and travel could be negatively impacted by political unrest and conflicts.

Border Disputes: Border restrictions could be the result of shifting borders and political rivalries, making it difficult to travel and conduct business.

Tribal Conflicts: Rivalries between nomadic peoples and local kingdoms occasionally broke out, putting the lives of caravans at risk.

7. Inadequate Infrastructure: Fewer Services

The Silk Road did not have the infrastructure or conveniences that modern highways and transportation networks do:

Travellers often had to make up with primitive inns or impromptu campsites that lacked the standard amenities seen in today's motels.

Herbal medicines and conventional treatments were about the extent of the available medical care along the Silk Road.

8. Difficulties in Finding Your Way Due to a Lack of Current Maps

Those who travelled the Silk Road made do with crude charts and compasses. Getting your bearings was a hassle before the advent of GPS:

Navigational Errors: In unfamiliar territory with few landmarks, getting lost is a real possibility for tourists.

Number Nine: The Dangers of Animals and Other Pests

There were many dangerous animals and insects along the Silk Road:

Travellers and their cattle may be at risk from predators like wolves and big cats in certain areas.

Tick-borne infections are just one example of the dangers posed by disease-carrying insects.

Despite the risks and difficulties, many people set out along the Silk Road in search of commerce, new cultures, and exciting experiences. These adventurers overcame the obstacles they encountered along the historic trade routes by working together and showing remarkable fortitude and resourcefulness. Modern-day explorers and researchers are motivated by their stories of adventure on the Silk Road to retrace their routes and learn more about the mysterious origins of this enduring emblem of human connection.

8.2- Efforts to overcome these challenges

It was a dangerous and difficult undertaking to travel the Silk Road. But throughout its extensive past, countless people and communities have shown extraordinary endurance and resourcefulness in the face of adversity. This research goes at the methods used by Silk Road travellers to overcome the obstacles they encountered.

1. Caravan Planning and Safety

Caravans, consisting of humans and pack animals like camels and horses, were one of the earliest forms of organised resistance to adversity. These caravans protected traders and their products from both human robbers and natural disasters.

Travellers knew there was strength in numbers and felt more secure. Large caravans were safer against robbers since they were less likely to attack a well-armed and numerous group of travellers.

Merchants and travellers frequently hired armed guards to go with the caravan. These guards scared away bandits and knew how to handle dangerous situations.

Camels, sometimes referred to as the "ships of the desert," served as indispensable pack animals for moving supplies across desert landscapes. They were able to haul big cargo, travel over sand, and stay on the road for days on end.

2. Diplomacy and Trade Agreements

Cooperation and diplomacy between cultures and states were necessary for trade along the Silk Road. Safe transit and easy trade were made possible thanks to diplomatic and commercial accords.

In order to ensure peaceful trade, several of the empires and nations located along the Silk Road formed treaties and commercial agreements. The protection of merchants and their merchandise was a common focus of these contracts.

Diplomatic Missions: Empires like the Roman and Han Empires despatched diplomatic missions to neighbouring states to foster cordial relations. There was political and economic motivation behind these missions.

Thirdly, Developments in Technology

Technologies that helped travellers deal with obstacles along the Silk Road were developed and spread during this time.

The camel saddle, for example, made travelling on camelback more convenient and efficient. In a similar vein, technological developments in shipbuilding have allowed for the construction of vessels that can safely traverse dangerous seas.

Travellers could better navigate and stay on course with the aid of navigational tools like compasses and astrolabes.

4. Cultural Interaction and Information Exchange

The dissemination of information is one of the Silk Road's most enduring legacies. Not only did they bring back material stuff, but also priceless knowledge.

Communication between people of different cultural backgrounds was greatly aided by the availability of guides and interpreters who spoke more than one language. Knowledge in subjects like physics, mathematics, and philosophy were able to be shared thanks to the translation of writings.

Diplomatic and Scholarly contacts: Scholars and intellectuals were frequently included in diplomatic missions, fostering intellectual and cultural contacts that benefited both parties.

5. Trading Posts and Urban Oases

Travellers along the Silk Road relied heavily on oasis cities and trading centres for shelter and supplies. These communities were set up in key locations to provide protection, resources, and commercial possibilities.

Caravanserais were rest stops along the route where travellers and their animals might stay the night. Within their sturdy walls, they provided food, lodging, and security.

Oasis cities' bazaars and marketplaces were important centres of commerce. They were hubs for the trading of products between different regions.

6. Adaptation and other Survival Strategies

To deal with the various hostile situations they encountered, Silk Road travellers came up with a wide variety of survival skills and strategies.

Travellers learnt to carefully manage their water supply by stocking up on water skins and finding safe refilling stations along their trip.

Clothing and housing were modified to better withstand the freezing weather. To combat the blazing heat of the day and the bone-chilling chill of the night, people wore multiple layers of clothes.

Long voyages necessitated the use of food preservation methods like drying and salting to guarantee a steady source of nourishment.

7. Mapping and Exploration

Exploratory voyages and endeavours to map and describe the Silk Road routes were frequently part of the efforts to overcome obstacles.

Mapping and Documentation: Explorers and travellers like Marco Polo and Xuanzang mapped and documented their itineraries. These writings were subsequently used by future travellers as reference materials.

Some trips along the Silk Road were undertaken for scientific purposes, with researchers and explorers gathering data about the region's topography, flora, wildlife, and cultures as they travelled.

8. Spiritual and Religious Guidance

Faith and spirituality provided comfort and strength for many vacationers. During difficult travels, many found solace and direction in their religious and spiritual practises.

Pilgrimage: Faith was a major source of strength for pilgrims making the dangerous journey along the Silk Road to see religious sites.

Religious Charities: Religious institutions along the Silk Road frequently assisted weary travellers by providing shelter, food, and medical care.

9 Capacity for Change and Recovery

The adaptability and resilience of Silk Road travellers was perhaps the most important aspect in overcoming obstacles. These people and their communities are inspiring in their resilience and ability to make do with what they have.

Risk Assessment: Seasoned explorers know how to weigh the benefits and drawbacks of many options before deciding whether to press on with a journey or turn back.

Loss of property, livestock, and even people due to bandit assaults or natural calamities required a high level of resilience. Despite difficulties, travellers persisted in their quests.

The Silk Road tested one's Endurance and Perseverance. It was common for travellers to endure exhausting treks, but they always knew that the final destination would be worth it.

Conclusion: Silk Road travellers used a wide variety of techniques, innovations, and adaptations to deal with the many difficulties they faced. Not only did these people and places show a strong passion for business, but they also shown an impressive aptitude for diplomacy, knowledge exchange, and the tenacity of the human spirit. The Silk Road is a symbol of the human spirit and the innumerable efforts people have made to reach across barriers and unite disparate communities and ecosystems.

Chapter 9.
Fall and History

9.1- Factors contributing to the decline of the Silk Road

An age of unmatched cultural exchange, business, and human interaction came to an end with the demise of the Silk Road, the historic network of trade routes that united East and West. This ancient network of commercial routes between China and the Mediterranean began to weaken for many reasons and eventually collapsed after flourishing for almost a millennium. In this analysis, we'll look into the main causes of the Silk Road's decline and fall.

One Major Change: The Development of Maritime Trade

The change in global trade routes was a major contributor to the extinction of the Silk Road. Overland commerce routes were abandoned in favour of marine ones as maritime technology advanced, making them safer and more efficient. Faster and cheaper alternatives to the Silk Road were made possible by the development of the Indian Ocean trade network and the discovery of new maritime routes around Africa, such as the Cape of Good Hope.

The Breakup of Governments and the Decline of Great Powers

Along the Silk Road, the political environment was shaped by the emergence and collapse of great empires. The fall of numerous major empires had a significant effect on international trade and cultural interaction:

The collapse of the Western Roman Empire in the fifth century CE greatly impacted Silk Road commerce. When the Roman Empire collapsed, it interrupted trade channels and reduced demand for Eastern luxury items.

The fall of the Han Dynasty in China, which occurred about the third century CE, led to political instability and division. Due to the ensuing periods of disintegration, trade and the upkeep of Silk Road routes were no longer centralised.

The Byzantine Empire, which had governed a sizable swath of territory around the western end of the Silk Road, eventually fell apart. The western Silk Road was significantly transformed in 1453, when the Ottoman Turks conquered Constantinople.

Third, geopolitical shifts have led to the emergence of new powers.

The geopolitical dynamics of the Silk Road changed as old empires fell and new countries and regional entities emerged.

Although the Mongol Empire—led by figures like Genghis Khan and Kublai Khan—made it easier for merchants to use the Silk Road during the Pax Mongolica, its subsequent dissolution into smaller Khanates led to a deterioration in centralised authority and security along the routes.

As European maritime powers like Portugal, Spain, and the Netherlands rose to prominence during the Age of Exploration, they looked for shorter, more direct ways to Asia by the sea rather than the longer, more circuitous Silk Road byway.

4. Economic Shifts: The Influence of Emerging Trade Products

Changes in economic climate and the introduction of novel commodities also contributed to the Silk Road's demise.

New Commodities Discovered: Silk Road goods lost some of their lustre once other markets were opened up, such as the Americas, and direct trade routes to spice-rich locations like the Moluccas were established.

Evolving Consumer Preferences: Consumers' changing tastes and the introduction of new items in Europe and Asia influenced shifts in demand. For instance, cotton and other textiles have overtaken silk in popularity.

5. The Effect of Technology on Modern Transportation

The demise of the Silk Road was hastened by the development of more efficient modes of transportation in the nineteenth and twentieth centuries.

Steamships and Railroads radically improved the efficiency, speed, and affordability of long-distance travel. These developments weakened the economic attractiveness of shipping goods via land.

The telegraph and other communication technologies eventually rendered the Silk Road obsolete, as they eliminated the need for long-distance trade caravans to transport messages and information.

Politico-Social Blockades and the Development of Isolationism

The free flow of products and people along the Silk Road was hampered by the closing of borders, the application of tariffs, and the growth of isolationist policies in various countries.

The Great Wall of China was built and expanded over many centuries to serve as a physical barrier to Silk Road trade as well as to demarcate state boundaries.

The adoption of protectionist trade policies by numerous empires restricted consumer access to foreign goods and stifled global commerce.

Natural barriers make up the seventh environmental factor.

The Silk Road's demise was hastened in no little part by environmental factors:

Climate Change: Droughts and changes in the courses of rivers, among other climatic changes, impacted agricultural production and water availability, which in turn impacted the feasibility of Silk Road routes.

The spread of deserts, such as the Taklamakan Desert, made some sites along the trade routes uninhabitable and presented difficulties for travellers.

8. Cultural and Religious Shifts: The Development of Islam

Cultural and religious shifts caused by Islam's propagation along the Silk Road influenced commercial activity:

As more and more places along the Silk Road converted to Islam, the Arab-Muslim world became more involved in maritime trade routes, resulting in deeper and more extensive ties between economies in the Indian Ocean.

9. Disease Epidemics: Plague and Pandemics

Deathly epidemics, such as the Black Death (bubonic plague) in the 14th century, hampered commerce and accelerated population loss along the Silk Road.

The destructive consequences of pandemic illness outbreaks on populations and the disruption of trade networks contributed to economic and social unrest.

10. The Effects of Colonial Powers on Culture and Society

Because of European imperial expansion in Asia, Africa, and the Americas, trade routes along the Silk Road were frequently rerouted.

European colonial powers took control of strategic commercial routes and resources, diverting commerce away from the Silk Road as a result.

In conclusion, the fall of the Silk Road was a multifaceted process affected by a wide range of interrelated elements, such as changing trade routes, shifting geopolitical power, developing technologies, overcoming environmental obstacles, and adapting to new economic and cultural conditions. Although the Silk Road is no longer the major means of international trade and cultural exchange, its historical legacy lives on as a symbol of human connectedness, perseverance, and the ever-present drive to learn and grow through experience.

9.2- The lasting legacy of the Silk Road on global trade and culture

The Silk Road, a historical network of trade routes connecting East and West, had a profound impact on international commerce and culture that is still felt today. Despite its collapse as a physical trade route, its legacy continues to affect the world in a variety of ways, including commerce, cultural interaction, and the dissemination of ideas. The Silk Road has left an indelible mark on international commerce and culture, and we'll examine that impact here.

1) Its Effect on Present-Day Trade Routes

The Silk Road has left a lasting impact on international trade today. The Silk Road paved the way for today's networks of shipping and aviation, which are essential to global trade. Important features of this heritage are:

Eurasian Integration: The Silk Road connected many different economies, and this concept of cooperation is important in today's global economy. This idea is now being put into action by projects like China's Belt and Road Initiative (BRI), which aims to revive the historic Silk Road trade routes.

The Silk Road altered the pattern of trade between the East and West. Even if individual trade routes have changed, the underlying dynamics of East-West commerce have not changed much throughout time.

Trading along the Silk Road facilitated significant cultural interactions. In a similar vein, modern trade encourages cultural exchanges, which in turn promotes the blending of diverse cultural expressions around the world.

2. The Maintenance and Renewal of Time-Honored Professions

The Silk Road was essential for the dissemination of creative works. Traditional crafts, especially in areas along its historic routes, continue to bear witness to its influence.

Trade in textiles, which became famous along the Silk Road, is still active today. The silk, cotton, and wool textile industries in places like India, China, and Central Asia are testaments to the ongoing impact of Silk Road customs.

Ceramics: There was a substantial trade in ceramics along the Silk Road. Countries like China and Iran have maintained their traditions of using and appreciating traditional ceramic processes, glazes, and designs.

Metalwork and Jewellery: The exquisite designs and techniques of metalwork and jewellery made along the Silk Road have left a lasting impact.

3. International Cooking and the Sharing of Recipes

The Silk Road was instrumental in the global dissemination of culinary customs and ingredients. The amalgamation of tastes and cuisines around the world is a testament to its influence.

Trade in spices, especially those from the East, radically altered Western culinary customs. Cinnamon, cardamom, and black pepper are still used often in kitchens all throughout the world.

Rice, wheat, and tea are just a few examples of the ingredients that made their way along the Silk Road and remain mainstays in the diets of billions of people today.

Modern cuisines are heavily influenced by the cooking methods and recipes that were traded over the Silk Road. The history of the dumpling, a dish common to many cultures, may be traced back to Silk Road commerce.

Knowledge and Information Propagation

The Silk Road served as a conduit for more than simply material commodities; it also served as a forum for the free flow of information, philosophy, and religion. The spread of ideas and innovations long after its death is a testament to its influence.

Cultures and societies were profoundly impacted by the introduction of Buddhism, Islam, Christianity, and other religions along the Silk Road. The world's spiritual and ethical landscape is still being moulded by these religions.

 Scientific and Technological Exchange: The Silk Road was a conduit for the dissemination of new ideas and inventions in the scientific, mathematical, and medical communities. This heritage is still present in cutting-edge research today.

Along the Silk Road, people shared works of literature, philosophical tracts, and creative techniques, all of which influenced the growth of literature and culture around the world.

5. Cultural Heritage and Travel

Travellers and academics from all over the world go to the areas along the Silk Road to learn about the region's rich history and culture.

Major tourist destinations have emerged along the Silk Road, including China's Great Wall, Jordan's Petra, and Uzbekistan's old city of Samarkand. The cultural and historical legacy of the Silk Road is protected at these locations.

Possibilities for Study and Investigation: The Silk Road's historical relevance is still being investigated, shedding light on ancient societies and their networks of commerce.

Reestablishing Connections and Commercial Trade Routes (No. 6)

The importance of restoring Silk Road economic connections has grown in recent years.

Through the construction of infrastructure, transportation networks, and commercial connections in Asia, Europe, and Africa, China's Belt and Road Initiative (BRI) aspires to revive and update the ancient Silk Road trade routes.

Trans-Eurasian Railway: Work is underway to set up efficient rail connections that cross the Eurasian continent, easing the transport of goods and people along lines reminiscent of the Silk Road.

Data, knowledge, and online trade have replaced the ancient Silk Road as the primary means of economic exchange in the modern day. The internet and other technologies have created a global trading network that is reminiscent of the ancient Silk Road.

7. International and Cultural Relations

Diplomatic and cultural relations between countries and regions are also a lasting result of the Silk Road:

Because of their common past and future economic interests, countries along the Silk Road have increased their diplomatic ties. Peace and cooperation are fostered by these linkages.

Cultural Diplomacy: Festivals, exhibitions, and other cultural exchange activities that honour the Silk Road's history promote international understanding and goodwill.

8. Thoughts About the Environment

There is now a rising consciousness of the negative effects of commerce and transportation on the natural world. Sustainable trade and transportation networks are being developed with the use of lessons learned from the Silk Road's history.

Initiatives are being made to create carbon-efficient transport systems, known as "green transport."

 harm to ecosystems, etc.

Sustainable agriculture (sometimes known as "green farming") is an emerging field that draws inspiration from traditional practises of trading agricultural goods.

In conclusion, the Silk Road has left an indelible mark on international commerce and culture. The loss of the physical trade routes has not diminished the impact of the ideas, goods, and cultural interaction that took place along them. The Silk Road is a symbol of the common human history of exploration, communication, and cooperation beyond national boundaries. We continue to benefit from its legacy, which sheds light on how past exchanges of goods and ideas shaped the current world.

Chapter 10.
Revival and rediscovery

10.1- Modern efforts to revive the Silk Road as a cultural and economic corridor

There has been a recent uptick in interest in restoring the Silk Road as a cultural and commercial corridor, with proponents hoping to restore the routes' original function as a means of commerce, communication, and cultural exchange. Infrastructure projects, diplomatic endeavours, cultural exchanges, and commercial ties are all part of the modern Silk Road revival movement. The goals of these initiatives are to increase cultural exchange and mutual understanding amongst countries that were once connected by the Silk Road. Here, we'll look into the modern initiatives that are making the Silk Road a more active cultural and economic corridor.

"The Belt and Road Initiative (BRI): A Vision for a 21st-Century Silk Road"

China's Belt and Road Initiative (BRI) is one of the most ambitious and visible endeavours to revitalise the Silk Road in the 21st century. The BRI is a comprehensive plan introduced in 2013 to improve communication and collaboration between nations in Asia, Europe, and Africa. The BRI plans to increase trade, infrastructure development, and cultural interaction by creating a contemporary Silk Road that includes both land and sea routes.

Massive infrastructure projects, such as the building of motorways, railways, ports, and energy pipelines, are at the heart of the Belt and Road Initiative (BRI). These initiatives aim to rebuild the infrastructure of the historic Silk Road, easing the movement of people and commerce across great distances.

The BRI promotes financial, commercial, and industrial cooperation among its member states. It promotes economic cooperation among member countries and attempts to ease commerce by lowering barriers and streamlining customs processes.

The BRI places a premium on cross-cultural communication and personal connections. It encourages collaboration in areas including tourism, archaeology, and heritage preservation as well as scholarly and cultural exchanges.

The New Silk Road and the Railways of Eurasia

Modern efforts to revitalise the Silk Road include building rail lines across Eurasia. These train routes between Europe and Asia are a speedier and greener option to shipping goods across the ocean. Among the more noteworthy endeavours are:

The Trans-Siberian Railway connects Moscow and Vladivostok and plays a crucial role in facilitating commerce and travel between Europe and Asia.

Trans-Eurasian Railway: The Trans-Eurasian Railway network is a collection of rail routes that spans Asia and Europe. This project's goal is to increase the productivity and volume of regional trade.

Freight trains that traverse the Eurasian continent are gaining popularity, and they are known as China-Europe Block Trains. The time it takes to move goods through these trains between Chinese cities and numerous European destinations is significantly less than via sea methods.

Third, the Conservation of Cultural Artefacts for Future Generations

Efforts to revitalise the Silk Road include protecting and sharing the route's cultural history. Important roles in this direction have been performed by archaeological investigations, preservation efforts, and the rise of cultural tourism.

Ongoing archaeological excavations along Silk Road routes have uncovered ancient artefacts, historical locations, and cultural remnants, providing new insights into the commerce and civilizations that flourished there in the past.

Silk Road heritage sites, such as the ancient city of Samarkand in Uzbekistan, the Mogao Caves in China, and Petra in Jordan, are the focus of conservation efforts. Many of these locations are recognised as World Heritage Sites by UNESCO.

Cultural Tourism: Many areas along the Silk Road have embraced cultural tourism, giving tourists the chance to learn about the region's rich history and unique culture. Cultural exchange and economic growth are both boosted by these programmes.

Fourth, the Digital Silk Road: Technology and Electronic Commerce

In today's digital era, a new Silk Road has emerged: the "Digital Silk Road." In its current form, it makes use of e-commerce, technology, and digital connection to promote commercial and cultural interaction:

E-commerce Platforms: E-commerce platforms and online marketplaces connect enterprises in Silk Road countries with customers all over the world.

Digital Payment Systems: The widespread adoption of digital payment systems has facilitated international trade by lowering transaction costs and increasing accessibility.

Blockchain Technology: Blockchain technology is being investigated as a way to improve supply chain security and transparency in cross-border trading along the Silk Road.

5. Diplomacy and International Organisations

Cooperation along the Silk Road is a priority for diplomatic initiatives and international organisations.

Sustainable development, cultural preservation, and regional collaboration along Silk Road routes are all priorities for the United Nations.

The Asian Infrastructure Investment Bank (AIIB): With an emphasis on infrastructure, the Asian Infrastructure Investment Bank provides funding for initiatives that improve trade along the new Silk Road.

In order to facilitate diplomatic collaboration, the resolution of conflicts, and the negotiating of commercial agreements, countries along the Silk Road engage in bilateral and multilateral discussions.

Initiatives in Higher Education and Related Fields (No. 6)

The revival of the Silk Road is largely dependent on academic institutions and educational programmes.

intellectual and cultural inheritance:

Scholarly Investigations: Academics study and write on the Silk Road's history, culture, and effect on international trade.

Educational Exchanges: Universities and institutions promote international collaboration and cultural understanding through student and teacher exchanges.

Seventh: Intercultural Communication and Travel

Mutual understanding and admiration between countries along the Silk Road are bolstered by cross-cultural exchanges and tourism programmes.

Countries along the Silk Road actively encourage cultural tourism by providing visitors with access to museums, historical landmarks, and unique ways of life.

Cultural interactions and international cooperation are encouraged by the prevalence of "sister city" relationships and partnerships between cities located along the Silk Road.

Sustainability and Environmental Factors

Reviving the Silk Road in the modern era also takes environmental concerns into account:

Some Silk Road infrastructure projects, such as those involving energy-efficient transit systems and eco-friendly urban development, are created with environmental sustainability in mind.

Ecotourism : Tourism activities that preserve natural areas and reduce their negative influence on the environment are supported.

Ultimately, the modern initiatives to resurrect the Silk Road as a cultural and commercial corridor are dynamic and involve many different fronts. Through increased communication, commerce, and understanding across nations, these projects want to revive the spirit of the original Silk Road. The legacy of the Silk Road continues to play a key role in determining the future of international relations, economics, and cultural understanding as the globe becomes more interconnected through digital technology and global trade. It's proof that ancient trade routes had a lasting effect on the modern economy.

10.2- Contemporary journeys and adventures along the ancient route

The Silk Road has always captivated the imaginations of intrepid explorers, curious scholars, and curious travellers, even if it is no longer the principal route for global trade and cultural exchange. Travelling the paths of the old Silk Road today is not just a reflection of the network's ongoing appeal, but also a way to renew the desire to learn about and appreciate other cultures. Some of the most incredible modern adventures and travels along the Silk Road will be the focus of this investigation.

1. Following in the Footsteps of the Ancients: Current Expeditions

Many modern day explorers and travellers go out to follow the steps of the ancient Silk Road. Contemporary explorers are interested in reestablishing a dialogue with the past by visiting archaeological sites and learning about the cultures that thrived along the old trade route. Among the most notable trips are:

The 2019 film Journey on the Silk Road: Levison Wood, a British explorer and adventurer, set out to follow the Silk Road's original route from Afghanistan to Greece. His journey spanned over four thousand kilometres of desert, mountain, and varied terrain.

The Silk Road Expedition (2020): A group of British explorers rode motorcycles from the United Kingdom to China via the ancient Silk Road. Their travels through a variety of landscapes and cultural settings are a testament to the allure of Silk Road discovery even today.

2. Artistic and Cultural Exploration

Travelling along the Silk Road is a popular pastime for modern artists and culture vultures who are interested in learning more about the region's rich history and fostering understanding amongst people of different backgrounds.

Several groups and institutions along the Silk Road have artists in residence and host cultural exchange programmes. Participating artists from the visual arts, music, and literature work together with their local counterparts to produce new works.

Countries everywhere along the Silk Road celebrate the rich cultural diversity of the region by hosting music and dance festivals. These gatherings celebrate the region's cultural legacy by showcasing both historical and modern artistic forms.

Thirdly, charitable and aid-oriented expeditions

Today's trips along the Silk Road aren't only about discovery and adventuring; they frequently serve charitable purposes as well.

Medical Expeditions : medical professionals and volunteers travel to underserved areas along the Silk Road to deliver medical aid. The medical needs and accessibility of healthcare are among the primary focuses of these missions.

Communities along the Silk Road often benefit from food, clothing, and medical supplies delivered by convoys organised by humanitarian organisations. Challenges like poverty and homelessness are being met thanks to these initiatives.

(4) Ecological and Nature-Based Travel Experiences

The Silk Road is a popular route for ecotourists since it winds through many different ecosystems.

Ecotourism initiatives encourage people to travel in a way that helps preserve the environment and gives back to local communities. Visitors to Silk Road countries participate in conservation efforts by doing things like watching local wildlife up close.

The Pamir Mountains, the Gobi Desert, and the Silk Road oases are just a few of the natural treasures that may be experienced during a journey along the Silk Road. The diverse landscapes of the region are highlighted on these treks.

5. Educational and Scientific Expeditions

In order to better comprehend the region's history, culture, and current concerns, academics, scholars, and researchers frequently travel along the Silk Road.

In order to better understand the ancient civilizations that flourished along the Silk Road, archaeologists conduct excavations and surveys along these routes. These explorations reveal previously unknown facts about the past.

Anthropologists, sociologists, and linguists, to name a few, conduct fieldwork along the Silk Road to learn more about modern societies and their languages. Their studies help fill gaps in the documentation of ongoing customs.

Ecological difficulties and preservation initiatives along the Silk Road are studied by environmental researchers. Their research contributes to conservation and development plans that are more environmentally friendly.

Sixthly: Exploration of the Silk Road and Extreme Tourism

Travellers in search of heart-pounding adventures and immersive cultural experiences have found a haven along Silk Road corridors.

Long-distance cyclists go to the Silk Road routes to take in the region's many landscapes and cultures on so-called "Silk Road Cycling Tours." These vacations have an exciting mix of cultural learning and outdoor fun.

The pathways of the Silk Road are popular destinations for hikers and trekkers who want to experience the region's wild landscape and pristine mountain regions. These trips allow you to spend time in the great outdoors and interact with the locals.

Off-Road Adventures: Off-road aficionados drive across difficult terrain in four-wheel-drive cars. These trips typically involve visits to off-the-beaten-path Silk Road locations.

7. Learning Opportunities and Exposure to Other Cultures

Silk Road study programmes and experiential learning opportunities are available from a variety of educational institutions and organisations along the route:

Institutions of higher learning provide study abroad programmes that emphasise the history, culture, and languages of the Silk Road.

Students are able to experience the rich cultural history of the region firsthand.

Learning the Languages Spoken Along the Silk Road: Mandarin, Mongolian, and Tajik Through Language Schools and Cultural Immersion Programmes Travellers Can:

Languages: Persian, Uzbek, and Turkish.

Documentary and Travel Writing about the Silk Road

Documentaries, books, and other forms of multimedia storytelling frequently feature modern itineraries along the Silk Road:

Documentary Films: Filmmakers capture their trips along the Silk Road, recording the sights, sounds, and people they encounter. The cinematic and narrative perspectives they offer on Silk Road travel are invaluable.

Travel Literature: Authors and other adventurers write about their experiences along the Silk Road for an international audience.

In conclusion, modern explorations of the old Silk Road demonstrate the route's continued allure and significance. These voyages, whether undertaken for exploration, cultural exchange, scholarly inquiry, or humanitarian ends, continue to encourage regional cooperation, honour the Silk Road's past, and foster cross-cultural understanding. They offer the next generation the chance to carry on the tradition of exploration and connection that has distinguished this ancient route for centuries.

Chapter 11.
Conclusion

11.1- Summarizing the key takeaways from the journey through Silk Road history

The Silk Road is a fascinating historical tour through a network of ancient trade routes that once linked East and West, allowing for the free flow of products, ideas, and religions. Several essential insights arise when we consider this incredible historical journey, all of which highlight the Silk Road's continuing importance:

(1) The Strength of Human Bonds

The Silk Road, at its heart, is a symbol of the unbreakable bonds between people. Over a thousand years of trade, diplomacy, and cultural contact between individuals of different ethnicities and socioeconomic backgrounds were on display. The Silk Road serves as a reminder that people have an innate propensity to reach out to others and learn from their experiences.

Syncretism and cultural interaction

The Silk Road's contribution to cross-continental cultural interchange and fusion is one of its most enduring legacies. Along its pathways, people traded more than just products; they also shared ideas, works of art, songs, and even religions. As a result of cultural exchange, many groundbreaking artistic movements, architectural feats, and philosophical concepts emerged.

Thirdly, Developments in Science and Technology

The Silk Road served as more than a commercial thoroughfare; it also promoted the exchange of ideas and innovations. Along the way, discoveries in areas as diverse as mathematics, astronomy, medicine, and engineering helped develop the state of knowledge and technology.

The Spread of Religion

Buddhism, Islam, Christianity, and Zoroastrianism, among others, all owe a great deal to the Silk Road for its global dissemination. The Silk Road serves as a reminder of the significance of religious pluralism and the transformative power of faith in moulding human culture and civilization.

Importance to the Economy, Number Five

The Silk Road's commercial activity served as the engine that propelled regional development and wealth. Economic growth was emphasised, along with the roles of trade, entrepreneurship, and new ideas. The Silk Road's teachings in commerce and enterprise are still applicable today.

Six The Rise and Fall of Great Powers

The geopolitical environment is always shifting, and the rise and fall of empires along the Silk Road is a prime example of this. The route's economic and cultural dynamics, as well as its safety, have fluctuated with the rise and fall of dynasties and empires from the Roman Empire to the Mongol Empire.

7. Enviornmental Difficulties

Travellers on the Silk Road faced enormous hurdles because to environmental conditions such as rough terrain, deserts, and changing river patterns. These difficulties serve as a timely reminder of the environmental influence on human civilization and the imperative for sustainable methods.

8. flexibility and toughness

Exploring the Silk Road's past exposes the incredible perseverance and adaptability of people who prospered in difficult settings. It stresses the value of being flexible and creative when facing challenges.

Reviving the Silk Road in the Twenty-First Century

The route's continued relevance is shown in modern efforts to revitalise it, such as China's Belt and Road Initiative. They show that the Silk Road's emphasis on communication, mutual understanding, and commerce has not been forgotten in the twenty-first century.

Globalization's Ten Greatest Lessons

The Silk Road can teach us a lot about living in a globalised society. It shows us how vital it is to learn from one another and communicate across cultural boundaries in today's interdependent and multicultural world. The Silk Road's lasting impact should inspire us to welcome difference and unite around a common goal of growth and prosperity.

In conclusion, learning about the history of the Silk Road is a fascinating look into the human desire to discover, trade, and share ideas and cultures. It's a reminder of the strength of interpersonal bonds, the value of interacting with people from different backgrounds, and the resilience of the human spirit in the face of adversity. The Silk Road's heritage encourages us to put aside our differences, honour those who are different from us, and work together to create a better, more peaceful world. Thinking on the Silk Road's history serves as a reminder that it is more than just a historical artefact; it is also a universal symbol of the human spirit's insatiable need for knowledge and its unyielding pursuit of new connections.

11.2- Reflection on the enduring importance of the Silk Road in today's world

It is impossible to overestimate the Silk Road's relevance to modern society. While the actual Silk Road trade routes have been lost to time, the legacy it left behind has had a lasting impact on the modern world. In this article, we'll look at how the Silk Road's ideals, principles, and spirit continue to reverberate in our modern, linked world.

The importance of cultural exchange and communication

Along the Silk Road, Eastern and Western civilizations collided, giving rise to a melting pot of customs, languages, and beliefs. This heritage of intercultural exchange is still crucial in the modern world. Because of globalisation, more people than ever before are able to meet others from diverse cultures, learn from one another, and develop an appreciation for one another's traditions. The Silk Road demonstrates the importance of embracing cultural differences for the greater good.

(2) Trade and Economic Integration

The Silk Road was an economic engine, connecting far-flung areas and fostering trade. International trade has always been crucial to the development of global economies, and this is true in the modern world. We may still learn from the Silk Road's examples of enterprise, creativity, and collaboration. The importance of trade routes and infrastructure projects in promoting economic integration is demonstrated by initiatives such as China's Belt and Road Initiative (BRI).

Thirdly, Globalisation and Connectivity

As a forerunner to modern globalisation, the Silk Road is an important historical link. Information, goods, services, and ideas are freely moving across boundaries in today's globalised society. The Silk Road serves as a sobering reminder that our interconnected society demands that we act morally and responsibly at all times.

4. Environmental Permanence

Travellers on the Silk Road had to adjust to a wide variety of environments, from deserts to mountains. The Silk Road serves as a modern-day allegory for the value of ecological balance. Climate change and resource depletion are two of the most urgent environmental problems the world currently faces. The Silk Road's legacy of toughness and flexibility teaches us the need of environmental protection and long-term planning.

5. Diplomacy and International Relations

The history of the Silk Road was deeply entangled with geopolitical shifts and diplomatic manoeuvring, as competing empires and states fought over control of vital trading routes. Diplomacy is still essential for keeping the peace and stability in today's world. The history of the Silk Road exemplifies the value of diplomatic channels for resolving international disputes.

6. Developments in Science and Technology

The Silk Road served as a conduit for the dissemination of new ideas and technological advancements. The speed with which technology is developing now is altering our economies and cultures. The Silk Road's historic function as a means of information dissemination motivates us to use technology for the common good and to tackle global problems.

7. Pluralism and tolerance in religions

The Silk Road was characterised by religious diversity, with different faiths coexisting and influencing one another. Religious pluralism is a fact of life in many modern nations. The legacy of religious tolerance left by the Silk Road serves as a reminder of the need to promote religious harmony and respect for all faiths.

8. Teaching and Exchanging Information

The Silk Road was instrumental in the spread of information and learning by allowing for the transport of books, manuscripts, and ideas. Education continues to be a potent force for both individual and societal development in today's world. The Silk Road's legacy compels us to place a premium on learning, stimulate intellectual curiosity, and disseminate information for the benefit of all.

9. Opportunities and Challenges

From natural disasters to political upheavals, the Silk Road's history was fraught with difficulty. Inequality, poverty, and the relocation of communities are just some of the new global concerns we confront today. The Silk Road serves as a reminder that obstacles may be overcome by creative problem solving, teamwork, and a dedication to human advancement.

10 Strength through Diversity

Silk Road's lasting legacy may be the idea of "unity in diversity." The Silk Road demonstrated the power of the human spirit to bridge linguistic, cultural, and religious divides. In order to solve global problems, spread peace, and create a more just and equitable society, it is crucial that we learn to work together despite our differences.

In conclusion, the Silk Road's continuing relevance in the modern world rests in its capacity to encourage us to prioritise mutual understanding, cooperation, and respect across cultures and beyond borders. It's a metaphor for the commonalities of our species and the unity of the human race. In order to honour the Silk Road's heritage, we must create a society that chooses unity over division, peace over war, and the well-being of all beings and the planet over personal gain. When we think about the Silk Road, we are reminded that it is more than just a historical route; it is also a beacon for our path forward, urging us to keep working towards peace, prosperity, and mutual understanding in a world that is constantly evolving.

Chapter 12.
Extra Materials

12.1- Suggestions for further reading and research

There is a multitude of books and materials accessible for individuals interested in learning more about the Silk Road and its historical, cultural, and philosophical significance. The suggested reading and study below spans a wide range of historical sources, contemporary studies, and multidisciplinary perspectives on the Silk Road.

1. Original Documents and Historical Accounts

- Peter Frankopan, "The Silk Roads: A New History of the World" An interesting and informative read that puts the Silk Road back at the centre of global events.

The classic account of Marco Polo's travels down the Silk Road in the 13th century, "The Travels of Marco Polo" by Marco Polo.

- Jack Weatherford's "The Secret History of the Mongol Queens" delves into the influence of women throughout Mongol history, including on the Silk Road.

- James A. Millward, "The Silk Road: A Very Short Introduction" This article provides a synopsis of the Silk Road's cultural and historical significance.

2) Delving into New Art Forms

Susan Whitfield, "Dunhuang: A City on the Silk Road" Dunhuang, a major stop along the Silk Road, is the subject of this lavishly illustrated volume.

Luce Boulnois's "Silk Road: Monks, Warriors & Merchants" delves at the cultural interactions that occurred along the Silk Road, including the spread of Buddhism and other faiths.

Frances Wood's "The Silk Road: Two Thousand Years in the Heart of Asia" is a beautiful coffee table book that explores the Silk Road through the lens of art and culture.

3. Scientific and Archaeological Investigations

Susan Whitfield's "The Archaeology of the Silk Road" provides an exhaustive survey of the findings from digs along the Silk Road that explain its past.

- "Silk Roads: The Routes Network of Chang'an-Tianshan Corridor" published by UNESCO: The work of UNESCO to conserve sites along the Silk Road is detailed in this publication.

John Hare's "The Desert Route to India" is a scientific investigation of the wildlife and vegetation along the Silk Road.

4. In the Present Day and Economically

An examination of China's Belt and Road Initiative (BRI) and its relevance to the modern world, "Belt and Road: A Chinese World Order" by Bruno Maçes.

Reference: Peter Frankopan, "The New Silk Roads: The Present and Future of the World" A sequel to "The Silk Roads," this time looking at how the Silk Road has changed in the twenty-first century.

5. Philosophical and Religious Considerations

Rupert Gethin's "The Buddhist Path to Awakening" delves at the cultural and social effects of Buddhism's spread along the Silk Road throughout history.

Buddhism had a significant impact along the Silk Road, and Dr. Laurel Marie Sobol's "Silk Road Wisdom: From 34 Buddhist Monks to 1200 Miracles" examines this phenomenon.

A look at how Islam was carried down the Silk Road and how it affected South Asia, "The Rise of Islam and the Bengal Frontier, 1204-1760" by Richard M. Eaton.

Current Journeys and Thrilling Adventures

Written by Helen Thayer, "Walking the Gobi: A 1,600-Mile Trek Across a Desert of Hope and Despair" is an exciting description of a contemporary trek through the Gobi Desert, an important Silk Road location.

A look at Kazakhstan, a country in the centre of the Silk Road, and its historical and cultural significance in "In Search of Kazakhstan: The Land That Disappeared" by Christopher Robbins.

7. Ecological and Long-Term Considerations

"The Great Derangement: Climate Change and the Unthinkable" by Amitav Ghosh is a look at the environmental problems in the Silk Road regions and how they relate to global warming.

Collection of essays by Anthony Reid and David Christian titled "The Silk Road and the Shaping of the Modern World" examines the environmental history of the Silk Road and its influence on the contemporary world.

Studies in Diplomacy and World Politics

Xinru Liu's "The Silk Road: A Political History" examines the geopolitical dynamics and the function of diplomacy along the Silk Road across time.

Firsthand tales of a Japanese priest's diplomatic journeys along the Silk Road in the 9th century; the book is titled "The Silk Road and Beyond: Narratives of a Priest on the Silk Road" by Jji Kawada.

9. Learning Materials and Digital Courses

Examine websites and establishments that host video lectures and courses about the civilizations and artefacts that may be found along the Silk Road. Coursera, edX, and Khan Academy are just a few online platforms that regularly feature such materials.

Ten. Galleries and Museums

Travel to locations that showcase the Silk Road's cultural and historical significance. There have been numerous Silk Road-themed exhibitions in museums such as the British Museum, the National Museum of China, and the Museum of Islamic Art in Qatar.

Explore scholarly publications, documentaries, and conferences dedicated to Silk Road studies in addition to the reading and study options given here. Silk Road studies can be approached from many different angles because of its interdisciplinary nature. The Silk Road's lasting significance offers a rich tapestry of knowledge to explore and admire, regardless of whether you're interested in history, culture, economics, or environmental issues.

12.2- Maps, illustrations, and photographs related to the Silk Road

We owe a great deal to the maps, illustrations, and photographs that have illuminated the Silk Road's topography, civilizations, and historical significance. These pictures have helped us find our way through the historic trade routes, picture the scenery, and value the works of art and architecture that sprang up along the way. We go into the realm of Silk Road-related maps, illustrations, and photographs, providing insights into how these visual representations have deepened our understanding of this cultural legacy.

First, a map showing the Silk Road's extensive network.

The complex network of trade routes that made up the Silk Road can only be understood with the use of maps. They provide an aerial perspective of the areas, settlements, and landmarks that merchants, tourists, and caravans have traversed for millennia. Notable Silk Road-related maps include:

- The Ptolemaic Map: Ptolemy's world map, which dates back to the 2nd century, has one of the first depictions of the Silk Road and includes extensive detail regarding cities and topographical features along the route.

The Star Chart of Dunhuang: This celestial chart, dating back to the 8th century and found in the Dunhuang caves, sheds light on how people living along the Silk Road in ancient China saw the night sky.

Numerous historical maps from different time periods, such as China's Tang Dynasty, Yuan Dynasty, and Ming Dynasty, shed light on the shifting Silk Road route network.

To aid in study and journey planning, modern cartographers have continued to create precise maps showing the Silk Road's ancient and present routes.

Second, the illustrations capture the splendour of Silk Road civilizations.

Artistic depictions and architectural blueprints alike have showcased the splendour and complexity of Silk Road civilizations. These images enrich our understanding of the cultural achievements, architectural marvels, and ordinary lives of the people who inhabit the areas along the route. Important examples include:

The complex pictures that cover mediaeval manuscripts from the Silk Road regions, such as illuminated Islamic manuscripts and Buddhist sutras, show scenes from sacred narratives and everyday life.

Explorers and travellers along the Silk Road, such as Marco Polo, frequently sketched the landscapes, cities, and people they visited, affording important glimpses into the past known today as travellers' sketches.

- Architectural Renderings: Architectural drawings and illustrations of Silk Road landmarks like the Mogao Caves in Dunhuang demonstrate the incredible creativity and workmanship of these historic locations.

Illustrations of the different artistic traditions and aesthetic sensibilities of the Silk Road region have preserved the unique textile patterns and artistic creations of the region.

Third, photographs offer a glimpse into the past along the Silk Road.

The significance of photography in recording the heritage, culture, and landscapes of the Silk Road has been revolutionary. Thanks to the development of photography in the 19th century, we have images that document the Silk Road's history and today. Among the most notable images are:

Documenting his travels along the Silk Road in the early 20th century, famed explorer Sven Hedin took photographs of uninhabited landscapes, ancient ruins, and local people.

- Photography by Aurel Stein: Aurel Stein, a pioneering archaeologist and explorer, took a large number of photographs at Silk Road locations during his explorations.

Photographers working today continue to record the landscapes and civilizations along the Silk Road, from the barren wastelands of Central Asia to the teeming souks of the Middle East.

Documenting Silk Road art and architecture as well as endangered cultural practises and artistic expressions, photography is an indispensable instrument in cultural preservation.

4. Electronic Reconstructions and Mappings

Digital mapping and 3D reconstructions have made it possible to create interactive and immersive Silk Road experiences. These technological aids provide an exciting new way to investigate landmarks and paths of the past:

Explore historical cities, temples, and archaeological sites along the Silk Road without leaving your home with the help of Virtual Silk Road Tours, an interactive online platform or app.

Digital reconstructions of Silk Road monuments using 3D modelling and reconstruction techniques allow scholars a glimpse into the buildings' former glory.

5. Displays and Collections in Museums

Extensive collections of Silk Road artefacts, maps, illustrations, and pictures can be found in museums all around the world. These collections are archival stores of historical information and cultural artefacts that allow visitors to have a personal connection to the Silk Road:

The British Museum in London is home to a wonderful collection of Silk Road artefacts, including textiles, manuscripts, and works of art.

The National Museum of China in Beijing hosts displays dedicated to the Silk Road that highlight the region's rich cultural heritage and artistic achievements.

The Met in New York City is home to a vast collection of Silk Road artefacts, including carpets and sculptures.

Academic journals and other scholarly publications (No.

Maps, graphics, and photographs frequently accompany research articles and historical analyses in academic journals and books devoted to the study of the Silk Road. Visual records of the Silk Road's impact are regularly updated by researchers and academics.

In conclusion, the contribution of Silk Road-related maps, pictures, and photographs to our knowledge of this ancient trading route is undeniable. With them, we can get an in-depth visual experience of the Silk Road's landscape, civilizations, and history. Researchers, teachers, and fans all benefit from these visual depictions, which deepen our understanding of the Silk Road's enduring legacy.

www.ingramcontent.com/pod-product-compliance
Lightning Source LLC
LaVergne TN
LVHW020448070526
838199LV00063B/4881